SPEAKING IN TONGUES

JESUS AND THE APOSTOLIC CHURCH AS MODELS
FOR THE CHURCH TODAY

SPEAKING IN TONGUES

JESUS AND THE APOSTOLIC CHURCH AS MODELS FOR THE CHURCH TODAY

Robert P. Menzies

CPT Press
Cleveland, Tennessee

Speaking in Tongues: Jesus and the Apostolic Church as Models for the Church Today

Published by CPT Press
900 Walker ST NE
Cleveland, TN 37311
USA
email: cptpress@pentecostaltheology.org
website: www.cptpress.com

Library of Congress Control Number: 2016934283

ISBN-10: 1935931563
ISBN-13: 9781935931560

DEDICATION

To my in-laws, Wayne and Doris Turnbull,

Pentecostal pioneers who have ministered in the joy and power of the Holy Spirit for over sixty years

TABLE OF CONTENTS

PREFACE

This book is the culmination of a spiritual journey. I began the journey as a young boy praying with my parents, brother, and many other 'brothers and sisters in the Lord' every Sunday evening at the altar of our home church. Those evening services always ended with an extended time of prayer kneeling together before God and calling out to him. It was in those moments of prayer that I first personally encountered God and witnessed firsthand his powerful presence. I remember with awe and affection those times of basking in the love of Christ and exulting in the joy of the Holy Spirit. Those experiences were often marked by fervent prayer, which routinely included inspired praise or intercession in tongues. This initial exposure to speaking in tongues left a deep, positive, and lasting impression upon me and encouraged me to experience this marvelous gift myself.

I vividly remember the night that I was baptized in the Holy Spirit and spoke in tongues like those early believers on the day of Pentecost (Acts 2.4). I was 13 years old and earnestly seeking God's promise (Acts 1.8). As I prayed in our church's prayer room at the conclusion of the service that night, I was caught up in the Lord's presence and overwhelmed by feelings of intense joy. I began to praise the Lord with words that did not conform to any language known to me. The words burst forth and for over an hour I was immersed in divine love and joy. A godly lady prayed with me that night and, after what must have been close to two hours, together we met my parents who were waiting for me. When this lady saw my father, she exclaimed, 'So this is your son!' She then explained that she too served at Evangel University, the school were my father taught. She described how earlier that day she had spoken with my father and felt led to pray for his son. That evening, unknown to her, she had again prayed for his son and her prayers were certainly answered.

These early experiences would serve as an indispensible measuring stick for my own spiritual and theological development. As I began to navigate the challenging world of academic study of the

Bible – a world often filled with skeptical presuppositions and critical assessments of the biblical accounts – this rich background of spiritual experience served me well. I look back on my time of study at Fuller Theological Seminary (MDiv) and then the University of Aberdeen in Scotland (PhD in New Testament Studies) with great fondness. I deeply appreciate the friends, professors, and churches associated with these schools and times of study. The process of learning and growth that I experienced during this period included exposure to many critical theories and perspectives that challenged the foundations of my faith. However, when doubts and confusion arose, I was constantly brought back to the bedrock basics – the Lordship of Jesus and the reality of his resurrection – by these rich, spiritual experiences, past and present. They reminded me of what was important and lasting, and they pointed me to the larger purposes of my own study and life: to glorify Jesus and bear bold witness for him.

My academic studies culminated in a PhD thesis that provided a framework for reassessing the New Testament teaching on the work of the Holy Spirit.[1] However, my focus in these early writings and research was on the nature of baptism in the Spirit (i.e. the Pentecostal gift of Acts 2) rather than speaking in tongues. In fact, I remember during this phase of my theological journey struggling with the doctrine of initial evidence. My struggles came to a head during Roger Stronstad's inaugural William Menzies Pentecostal Lectureship at Asia Pacific Theological Seminary (Baguio City, The Philippines) in 1993. Roger's lectures were great and inspiring. I, however, participated in a panel discussion that was less spectacular. A group of pastors present asked for a clear, biblical basis for the Pentecostal understanding of tongues as the initial, physical evidence of baptism in the Holy Spirit. As I recall, I struggled to provide compelling answers to the questions that were raised.

My experience at the lectureship challenged me to examine the initial evidence doctrine and my own theology of tongues more seriously. The result was a chapter entitled 'Evidential Tongues' that appeared in the book that I co-authored with my father, *Spirit and*

---

[1] This was published as *The Development of Early Christian Pneumatology with Special Reference to Luke–Acts* (JSNTSS 54; Sheffield: JSOT Press, 1991) and later, in a revised form, as *Empowered for Witness: The Spirit in Luke–Acts* (JPTSup 6; Sheffield: JSOT Press, 1994).

Power: Foundations of Pentecostal Experience (Zondervan, 2000). In this essay I argued that the doctrine of tongues as the initial evidence of baptism in the Holy Spirit flowed from a synthesis of theological insights offered by Luke and Paul. Thus, this doctrine was really the fruit of systematic reflection rather than biblical theology. More specifically, I argued that although none of the biblical writers consciously sought to teach this doctrine, it is an appropriate inference drawn from the fact that Luke, on the one hand, presents tongues as a sign of baptism in the Holy Spirit and that Paul, on the other, tells us that tongues is an edifying gift that is available to every believer. The central question for me that had not been adequately acknowledged or addressed by Pentecostals was this: while Luke clearly presents speaking in tongues as a sign of baptism in the Holy Spirit, does his narrative suggest that every believer should expect to manifest this sign? I concluded that Luke left this question unanswered, but that Paul provided what was needed: a clear affirmation that the gift of tongues is available to every believer (see 1 Cor. 12.30; 14.5, 18; and Chapter 5 below).[2]

Although I found this answer to the initial evidence question satisfying, nagging questions still lingered. If the doctrine of evidential tongues is an inference drawn from the contributions of Luke and Paul, then the significance of this systematic reflection must still be assessed. In other words, if this doctrine flows from our question rather than that of the biblical authors, one might legitimately ask just how significant this question is. I once again began to question my own assessment of the significance of tongues for individual Christians and for the gathered community.

This period of 'cautious acceptance, but lingering questions' came to an end in 2011. In that year I was asked to present two lectures on speaking in tongues to a group of Pentecostal pastors in Taiwan. Due to limited theological library resources in China, I spent a week in Hong Kong preparing for this time of ministry in Taiwan. My initial plan was to present one lecture on Luke's perspective on tongues and one lecture on Paul's perspective. However, as I began once again to examine Luke's narrative, I quickly found that I would barely have time to cover all that I found there

---

[2] Chapter 5, 'Paul: Tongues for Every Believer', first appeared in a slightly altered form in William Menzies and Robert Menzies, *Spirit and Power: Foundations of Pentecostal Experience* (Zondervan, 2000), pp. 133-44.

in both lectures. It was during this time of study that several texts, generally overlooked in this discussion, changed my perspective. The key texts that served as a catalyst for change were Lk. 10.1-17; 11.9-13; and the linguistic connections between Acts 2.4; 10.46; 19.6 (see Chapters 1 and 2 below).[3] As a result of this period of study I became firmly convinced that Luke had carefully crafted his narrative to encourage his readers – every one – to experience a baptism in the Spirit, a prophetic enabling (Acts 2.17-18), marked by speaking in tongues. Whereas in the past I had felt that none of the biblical authors consciously sought to teach tongues as a sign that should be expected by every Spirit-baptized believer, now I became convinced that this judgment was overly hasty and did not do justice to Luke's narrative.

This time of study in 2011 marked a new phase in my spiritual journey with reference to tongues. I became more conscious of this wonderful gift and emphasized its benefits more in my ministry in China. I would note that, where as a young boy my perspective on tongues began with experience and then moved to the Scriptures, as a mature adult the progression was different. My reading of Scripture challenged me to enlarge my vision and encouraged my experience.

This more recent 'confident and expectant' phase has also been enriched by my research and writing on Jesus' experience as recorded in Lk. 10.21 and Acts 2.26 (see Chapter 3 below).[4] Insights from these texts led me to consider more carefully Jesus' words recorded in the long ending of Mark (see esp. Mk 16.17-18 and Chapter 4 below), which has also served to fan the flame in my own life. This in turn led me to reconsider Paul's teaching on tongues, particularly his insights into tongues as a form of Spirit-inspired prayer and praise (see Chapters 6 and 7 below).

So, the following book is actually a kind of spiritual diary, one that chronicles my own journey into the riches of Spirit-inspired prayer and praise that issue forth in glossolalia. I had not intended to write a book focused exclusively on tongues. In fact, some years

---

[3] Chapters 1 and 2 represent edited versions of material (pp. 67-101) excerpted from *Pentecost: This Story Is Our Story* by Robert P. Menzies. Copyright © 2013 by Robert P. Menzies. Used by permission of Gospel Publishing House.

[4] Chapter 3 first appeared as Robert Menzies, 'Jesus, Tongues, and the Messianic Reading of Psalm 16', *JPT* 23.1 (2014), pp. 29-49.

ago I rejected a proposal to do something similar. I was fearful that this sort of book might be misunderstood and misused to foster unflattering caricatures of Pentecostals as people obsessed with speaking in tongues. However, I believe that my earlier writings provide a broader context for this book.[5] They demonstrate that Pentecostals are rooted in the Bible and focused on exalting Jesus. Speaking in tongues is merely one expression of the life of Christ in us, which we experience through the Holy Spirit. Well, I have overcome my fears. It is my hope that this book will encourage you to do so as well.

I would like to express my special thanks to Grant Hochman and Robert Graves. Both Grant and Robert carefully read my entire manuscript and offered extremely helpful comments. Their editorial notes helped me strengthen my presentation at numerous points. As one of my daughters pointed out, '[I am] greatly blessed to have friends like this'. Thank you, Grant and Robert, for your exceptional editorial skills and your willingness to labor long hours in order to help me produce a better book.

---

[5] See especially *Spirit and Power: Foundations for Pentecostal Experience* and *Pentecost: This Story Is Our Story*.

INTRODUCTION

My Chinese friends like to contrast 'chicken heart (*ji xin*) faith' with 'lion heart (*shi zi xin*) faith'. A lion's heart is much bigger than the tiny heart of a chicken. So, the saying is easy to understand. 'Chicken heart faith' refers to those of little faith, to those who are timid and fearful. By way of contrast, 'Lion heart faith' refers to those who are confident in the power of God and His leading. It speaks of those who are bold and courageous. When it comes to speaking in tongues, I feel that many Pentecostals in the United States have developed a bad case of 'chicken heart faith'. Let me explain.

From its beginnings at the Azusa Street Revival (1906–1909), speaking in tongues played an important role in the formation of the modern Pentecostal movement. This is no small matter, for the Pentecostal movement has been labeled by at least one sociologist as 'the most successful social movement of the past century'.[1] Since its humble beginning in a storefront mission, the movement has birthed dynamic churches around the world and now numbers around 300 million.[2] In a manner similar to the apostolic church (Acts 2, 10, 19), speaking in tongues has marked the experience and dynamism of this powerful Christian movement. It is an experience that in many respects helped shape and define the movement. In fact, a number of historians believe that without the connection between speaking in tongues and baptism in the Holy Spirit there

---

[1] Philip Jenkins, *The Next Christendom: The Coming of Global Christianity* (Oxford: Oxford University Press, 2002), p. 8.

[2] The Pew Research Center's Report on Global Christianity issued in December of 2011 stated that there were, at that time, just under 280 million denominational Pentecostals globally and 584 million Pentecostals and charismatics worldwide (http://www.pewforum.org/2011/12/19/global-christianity-exec/).

would be no modern Pentecostal movement.[3] I believe this judgment is correct.

The Significance of Tongues for the Modern Pentecostal Movement

One could undoubtedly name many reasons for the prominent role that speaking in tongues has played in the life of this dynamic movement, but two are especially significant. The first reason has to do with the way that Pentecostals read the Bible; the second with their unique evangelistic or missiological focus. Let's begin with the first reason.

We Pentecostals have always read the narrative of Acts, and particularly the account of the Pentecostal outpouring of the Holy Spirit (Acts 2), as a model for our own lives. We find encouragement in the way that God uses 'unschooled' and 'ordinary' people to advance His cause. We revel in stories of simple fishermen who are called and enabled to bear bold witness for Jesus. We delight in the account of poor peasants persevering in the midst of great opposition and suffering. These stories become our stories and encourage us also to live lives marked by extraordinary faith, the willingness to hazard risks, and a deep desire to exalt the name of Jesus. Around the world Pentecostals identify with these stories, especially since so many face similar challenges. This sense of connection with the text encourages us to allow the narrative to shape our lives, our hopes and dreams. So, we eagerly read these stories with a deep sense of expectation.

This simple, narrative approach to the book of Acts is one of the great strengths of the Pentecostal movement.[4] It is undoubtedly a large reason for its rapid growth around the world. The simplicity of reading the text as a model for our lives, without angst about the miraculous or how it all fits together into complex theological sys-

---

[3] Vinson Synan, 'The Role of Tongues as Initial Evidence', in Mark Wilson (ed.), *Spirit and Renewal: Essays in Honor of J. Rodman Williams* (JPTSup 5; Sheffield: Sheffield Academic Press, 1994), p. 82.

[4] Amos Yong views the Pentecostal approach to Acts as a helpful reminder 'that all narratives are didactic in some respect' (*The Spirit Poured Out on All Flesh. Pentecostalism and the Possibility of Global Theology* [Grand Rapids: Baker, 2005], p. 86).

tems clearly enables the message to be readily grasped by people in pre- or semi-literate cultures, people that are more experiential than cognitive in their orientation. We should not forget that these people represent the majority of the inhabitants of our planet. They too exhibit little concern about stories filled with miracles, but rather readily identify with them.

I also believe that this simple hermeneutic, this straightforward approach to reading Acts as a model for the church today, is one of the key reasons why an emphasis on speaking in tongues played such an important role in the formation of the modern Pentecostal movement. Certainly it has enabled Pentecostals to read the book of Acts without the preconceived notions that lead many Christians to limit tongues to the apostolic age. Yet equally significant is the way in which the experience of tongues affirms and validates this Pentecostal reading of the Bible and especially the book of Acts. When Pentecostals speak in tongues, this event serves as proof that the experience of the apostolic church, along with its calling and power, is indeed available today. Our own encounter with this dramatic, unusual experience described in the pages of Acts validates our hermeneutic and calls us to identify with the stories there that we read. The experience reinforces our sense of expectation. So, understandably, for Pentecostals Acts is not simply a historical document; rather, Acts presents a model for the life of the contemporary church. In short, speaking in tongues serves as a sign that 'their experience' is 'our experience' and that the pages of Acts should serve as our guide.

This leads us to the second reason that tongues has marked and shaped the Pentecostal movement. Speaking in tongues not only embodies and validates our reading of the Bible, it also calls us to recognize who we are. It calls the church to recognize and remember its true identity. It reminds us that we are nothing less than a community of end-time prophets called and empowered to bear bold witness for Jesus (Acts 2.17-21). On the Day of Pentecost those first-century disciples of Jesus were miraculously enabled to declare 'the wonders of God' in the various mother tongues of all those present. Luke describes this remarkable experience with these words: 'All of them were filled with the Holy Spirit and began to speak in other tongues as the Spirit enabled them' (Acts 2.4). Although this is probably the only instance in the New Testament where speaking in tongues is manifest as xenolalia – the miraculous, spontaneous ability to speak a previously unknown human language – this remarkable linguistic miracle is filled with symbolic significance. It serves to remind the early church and the readers of Acts, as well as subsequent generations of Christian tongues-speakers, that the church is called to cross every linguistic and cultural barrier in its quest to bear bold witness for Jesus to the ends of the earth. Little wonder, then, that the modern Pentecostal movement has been marked, not simply by speaking in tongues, but also by a remarkable missionary zeal. While this passion for sharing the good news of Jesus with others is energized by the Holy Spirit, it is symbolized and embodied in the experience of speaking in tongues. Every private and communal experience of glossolalia serves to remind the individual believer and the larger church body of the calling that we all have received and the enabling that we all have been promised (Acts 1.8). For Pentecostals, then, tongues serve as a sign that the calling and power of the apostolic church are valid for contemporary believers.

The Three Fears

In spite of the central role that speaking in tongues has played in the formation of the Pentecostal movement, I fear there is a growing tendency, at least in the United States, for Pentecostal pastors to downplay this dimension of Pentecostal theology and practice.[5] There are undoubtedly many reasons for this trend, but I would suggest that the key reason is fear.

Some years ago a Chinese house church leader, Brother Zhang, spoke in a chapel service at our Bible school. After an inspiring service, he met personally with Sister Mei, who explained that she felt called to take the gospel to her people, a largely Muslim group. I still remember Brother Zhang's words of exhortation. He said there are 'three fears' that you must overcome if you are to share the gospel with your people. First, don't be afraid of 'poor living conditions'. Second, don't be afraid of 'difficult work' (that is, ministering

---

[5] According to a 2006 Pew Research survey, 49% of Pentecostals in the U.S. say they have never spoken in tongues (http.//www.pewforum.org/files/2006/10/pentecostals-08.pdf).

among unresponsive people). Finally, don't be afraid of 'going to prison'. He concluded, 'If you overcome these fears, the Lord will use you in a powerful way'. Sister Mei was greatly encouraged by these sobering words. I, conversely, was amazed at how different his words of ministerial advice were from anything that I had heard in the West; this, in spite of the fact that they seemed to echo the words of the apostles.

Well, I also have my list of 'three fears' that I believe pastors need to overcome if they want their churches to experience the joy and power of speaking in tongues, and in so doing recapture the power of Pentecost and follow in the apostolic model. First, we need to overcome the fear of disagreement. Many pastors are simply afraid that if they preach on and encourage the experience of tongues, some in their church will disagree and leave. This fear is rooted in a lack of confidence. Can I present clear and convincing reasons for the link between baptism in the Spirit and speaking in tongues? Can I offer a biblical rationale for encouraging every believer to seek and experience this gift? I believe that many of our pastors have lost the sense of confidence at this point that marked earlier generations of Pentecostal leaders. I will explain why this is the case below.

The second fear is simply this: the fear of embarrassment. Many pastors are fearful that if they preach about tongues and proclaim the biblical promise, that God won't show up. They are fearful that their congregation will flock to the altar in anticipation, but that they will leave disappointed. It's a risky thing to proclaim that the experience of the apostolic church is available today. It's a risky thing to encourage our churches to seek the power of the Holy Spirit. We are not always sure what will happen because we are no longer in charge. It also takes time and energy to wait in the presence of the Lord for His power to fall like it did on the day of Pentecost (Acts 1.14; 2.1). In our time-conscious society, many of us are not willing to wait. After a few minutes we become uncomfortable and look to the pastor for further instruction. We have lost the ability to wait and pray. The pressure that the pastor feels is thus intensified. If something dramatic doesn't happen quickly, he will lose face.

The fear of embarrassment is particularly acute when it comes to speaking in tongues. After all, this experience is rather unusual.

While it may not be irrational, it does transcend our understanding. Additionally, how will those who are new to the church respond? Many might associate speaking in tongues with banjos, rural mountain churches, and the handling of snakes (Mk 16.17-18). Doesn't Paul encourage us to limit the corporate expression of this potentially misunderstood gift (1 Cor. 14.23-28)? No, surely this experience is best left to our private prayer closets. Shouldn't tongues be a matter of personal preference, discretely discussed outside our larger meetings?

Finally, there is also the fear of 'wild fire' or excess. Paul struggled with 'wild fire' at Corinth. The church there clearly was out of control (1 Cor. 14.20-28). If we encourage the gift in our churches, won't we face similar problems? And how does this fit with our new efforts to make 'seekers' feel welcome? Won't newcomers be put off by all of this? In light of the potential problems, surely it's better not to highlight this exotic experience.

These three fears are the reason that I have written this book. All of them are understandable, but all of them miss vital aspects of biblical teaching. I also think it is important for Pentecostals not to forget our rich heritage and recent history. You see, the early Pentecostals were also initially ridiculed for their doctrine and practice, which obviously included speaking in tongues. Just as in their minds speaking in tongues embodied and validated important aspects of their hermeneutic and theology, so also it became a lightning rod for criticism and ridicule. However, they were largely unfazed. They stood firm on the Scriptures, for they rightly recognized that this experience was widespread in the apostolic church, experienced by subsequent generations of believers,[6] and encouraged in the New Testament. Of course, they experienced a certain amount of 'wild fire'. The risks are real. Nevertheless, with the help of godly leadership and a clear grasp of biblical teaching, they successfully navigated these small storms. The result is clear to see: empowered by the Holy Spirit, an unlikely group of largely ordinary people

---

[6] Gary S. Shogren, 'The Gift of Tongues in the Post-Apostolic Church: A Rejoinder to Cleon Rogers', in Robert W. Graves (ed.), *Strangers to Fire: When Tradition Trumps Scripture* (Woodstock, GA: The Foundation for Pentecostal Scholarship, 2014), pp. 399-410.

launched a movement that has produced 'the greatest evangelism that the world has ever seen'.[7]

It is a risky thing to encounter God. Speaking in tongues symbolizes this risk, for it requires that we surrender control of that most significant and defining organ of our body, our tongue (Jas 3.1-12; Prov. 18.21). We are led to engage in actions that transcend our understanding and that may be incomprehensible to those around us. We might look and sound foolish to others and incur ridicule. Nevertheless, I would submit that the promise of God is worth hazarding the risk.

Facing Our Fears

How, then, shall we face these fears? I believe that courage flows from a strong sense of conviction, a clear apprehension of our call. The three fears can all be faced if we simply have a clear understanding of the biblical mandate. I noted above that many of our pastors have lost the confidence that marked earlier generations of Pentecostal leaders. Simply put, they no longer feel that they can proclaim with confidence that speaking in tongues is an experience that every believer can and should experience. Why is this the case? What has changed?

Historical Developments

Uncertainty or confusion regarding the biblical basis for a Pentecostal approach to speaking in tongues certainly afflicts many contemporary Pentecostal pastors and churches. This confusion is the result of an historical process that has been at work since the middle part of this past century: the assimilation of the Pentecostal movement into mainstream Evangelicalism. This process of assimilation, although gradual and unobtrusive, has significantly impacted the theology and practice of both the Evangelical and Pentecostal movements.[8]

---

[7] This quote comes from the pledge made by the delegates of the 2nd General Council of the Assemblies of God in 1914 (General Council of the Assemblies of God, *General Council Minutes [Combined Minutes], 1914-1917*, pp. 9-10).

[8] See Menzies, *Spirit and Power*, pp. 37-45, for a more detailed description of the impact this process of assimilation had on the way Pentecostals read the Bible as well as more recent, positive developments.

The theological roots of the Pentecostal movement are firmly planted in the nineteenth-century Holiness movement and American revivalism. This fertile soil nurtured the fundamental affirmations that characterize Pentecostal theology and the approach to Scripture upon which they stand.[9] These theological affirmations were, for a variety of reasons, produced in isolation from other sectors of the Christian community. However, with the advent of the Second World War, this quickly changed. Pentecostals frequently found themselves in close proximity to their Evangelical brothers and sisters. New relationships developed, fostering an atmosphere of openness. The Pentecostal movement rapidly began to identify with the broader Evangelical world. Pentecostal Bible colleges featured textbooks produced by Evangelical scholars; their students flooded into Evangelical seminaries. Evangelical institutions and publications impacted the ethos of Pentecostal churches and significantly influenced the outlook of the laity. Now, just over a century after its genesis, the Pentecostal movement finds itself in a new environment. American revivalism has given way to modern Evangelicalism. The major tenets of Pentecostal theology remain the same; but the way we as Pentecostals approach Scripture – the hermeneutic which supports our theology – has been significantly altered. The hermeneutic of Evangelicalism has, to a significant degree, shaped and become our hermeneutic.

The newly adopted Evangelical hermeneutic supports most of the theological doctrines Pentecostals hold dear – those we share with our Evangelical brothers and sisters.[10] Yet this hermeneutical shift has, in some instances, represented a very real challenge to those doctrines distinctive to Pentecostalism. This is especially true of the Pentecostal belief that baptism in the Spirit is an experience subsequent to (or distinct from) conversion and that glossolalia represents its initial physical evidence. These cardinal doctrines, formulated prior to the assimilation of the Pentecostal movement into the

---

[9] See Menzies, *Pentecost: This Story Is Our Story*, for a concise explanation of core Pentecostal beliefs and practice.

[10] Although Pentecostals represent a diverse sub-group within Evangelicalism, for the purpose of this book we shall distinguish between Pentecostals (assuming their identification with traditional Evangelical values) as those who affirm a baptism in the Spirit subsequent to conversion that is marked by speaking in tongues and Evangelicals as those who do not subscribe to this view.

larger Evangelical community, are based on an approach to Scripture that is not compatible with some versions of the new hermeneutic shaped by Evangelicalism. Thus, Pentecostal ministers occasionally find themselves espousing a theology that is based on an approach to Scripture that a significant portion of their congregation may not accept as valid.

The Way Forward

However, it should be noted that the influence has actually been mutual. Just as Evangelicals have influenced Pentecostals, so also have Pentecostals impacted the Evangelical movement. This Pentecostal influence is now conspicuous in the theological arena.

I have argued elsewhere that, ironically, due to their isolation, Pentecostals were enabled to make an important contribution to the larger church world.[11] Protestant theology, under the influence of Luther and Calvin, had been largely reduced to Pauline theology. The richness of these wonderful Pauline insights should not be minimized. Nevertheless, the New Testament canon is a bit larger than Paul's epistles. Through their simple, narrative approach to the book of Acts, Pentecostals have been able to integrate Luke's significant insights together with those of Paul, John, and the other inspired writers of the New Testament. The result has been a fuller, more holistic reading of the New Testament.

Additionally, I have noted that Pentecostals have been at the forefront of attempts to refine Evangelical approaches to the interpretation of the Bible.[12] As a result, we Pentecostals are enabling our Evangelical brothers and sisters to recognize the theological significance of biblical narratives and thus to benefit from the important, Spirit-inspired insights that flow from them. All of this bodes well for the future of the Pentecostal movement, but it takes time for these contributions to filter down and impact people in the pew. This is especially true of our attitudes toward speaking in tongues. When it comes to speaking in tongues, due to the historical process outlined above, our theology and practice often reflect older, outdated, and restrictive Evangelical attitudes. Thus there is a tension between our stated doctrine and our internal perceptions.

---

[11] Menzies, *Pentecost: This Story Is Our Story*, pp. 22-39, 117-26.

[12] Menzies, *Spirit and Power*, pp. 37-45 and Menzies, *Pentecost: This Story Is Our Story*, pp. 22-39.

The result is an understandable lack of confidence on the part of pastors and indifference in the pews. Sadly, in some quarters, we are perilously close to losing an important part of our heritage.

In order to recapture the confidence and wisdom of those early Pentecostal pioneers, we need to take a fresh look at the relevant Scriptures. And we need to do so with the recognition that Luke has a lot to contribute to this discussion. Indeed, in the pages that follow I will suggest that past discussions of speaking in tongues have largely ignored, for one reason or another, important texts in the Gospel of Luke and, in one instance, in the Gospel of Mark. Additionally, following the lead of a previous generation of Evangelical scholars, we have tended to give priority to Paul's teaching on the subject, even though his directives are aimed at correcting abnormal and problematic abuses. We have, at a number of points, largely ignored the contributions of Luke. I would also note that, due to presuppositions shaped by our own experience and patterns of worship, we have often missed or minimized the rich contribution that Paul has to make to this discussion as well.

With this fresh agenda in mind, I wish to take you on a journey through the New Testament teaching on speaking in tongues. I pray that you will be encouraged, informed, and inspired as you read the biblical texts with an open heart and mind. As we do, I believe that a fuller, more holistic theology of speaking in tongues will emerge: a theology that will serve to enhance our experience of God and inspire our service for Him.

Application

In an important essay, historian Vinson Synan highlights the significant role that speaking in tongues played in the development of the modern Pentecostal movement.[13] He notes that, 'for Pentecostals glossolalia was not only proof of the baptism in the Holy Spirit, but also was a repeatable evidence of the Holy Spirit's continued presence'. Additionally, the expectation of this experience encouraged 'all Pentecostals to seek a spiritual breakthrough'.[14]

---

[13] Synan, 'Role of Tongues', pp. 67-82.
[14] Synan, 'Role of Tongues', p. 75.

Synan makes an interesting observation: 'the Pentecostal churches that have held strongly to this teaching [initial evidence] have
surpassed all others in church growth and missionary success in the
period since World War II'.[15] He compares the Church of God in
Christ (COGIC) and the Church of Christ (Holiness). These two
groups separated in 1908 over the issue of tongues, with the former
affirming the experience and the latter rejecting the Pentecostal emphasis. At that time, both groups were roughly equal in size. Synan
states, 'By 1990 the church that rejected tongues as initial evidence
numbered only 15,000 members in the USA while the COGIC had
grown to number 3.7 million members'.[16]

Synan also compares the Assemblies of God (AG) and the
Christian Missionary Alliance (CMA). While the AG affirmed the
Pentecostal perspective on tongues, the CMA rejected it. The CMA
adopted the 'seek not, forbid not' policy and this 'effectively ended
the Pentecostal renewal in the CMA church'.[17] The results are instructive. 'By 1992 the CMA had grown to 265,863 members in the
USA and an estimated 1.9 million members around the world. On
the other hand, the Assemblies of God … had grown by 1992 to
2,170,890 members in the USA with an estimated worldwide con-
stituency of 25 million members'.[18] The Assemblies of God now
numbers 67 million adherents worldwide, with 3.1 million located in
the U.S.[19]

Synan concludes with these stirring words:

> In the end, the teaching of tongues as initial evidence has played
> a major role in recent church history. The Pentecostal experience
> and the doctrine explaining it has galvanized the most explosive
> movement among Christians since the days of the Reformation.
> It is unthinkable that the Pentecostal movement could have de-
> veloped as it did without the initial evidence position. The fact is
> that this teaching led millions of Christians to receive dramatic
> and life-changing experiences of baptism in the Holy Spirit,

---

[15] Synan, 'Role of Tongues', p. 81.
[16] Synan, 'Role of Tongues', p. 81.
[17] Synan, 'Role of Tongues', p. 81.
[18] Synan, 'Role of Tongues', p. 81.
[19] Assemblies of God 2013 Statistical Report, accessed online August 25,
2015 at http://ag.org/top/about/statistics/index.cfm.

which has led to an explosion of all the other charismata in the lives of Spirit-filled believers. The final and most important outcome may be the incredible growth of worldwide evangelization that has resulted from the charismatic manifestations of signs and wonders in many nations of the world.[20]

Why would Pentecostals in the West, and especially the U.S., move away from a doctrine and experience that have served us so well over the years? I believe that it is time to reconsider our willingness to embrace more trendy, 'seeker-sensitive' approaches to church life that in many instances leave little room for speaking in tongues, especially in the corporate setting.[21]

Reflection Questions

1. The author suggests that speaking in tongues has been important for Pentecostals the world over for many reasons, but two are of particular importance. What are these two reasons?

2. Menzies argues that three fears often keep pastors from speaking about or encouraging speaking in tongues. Do you agree?

3. According to the author, speaking in tongues involves taking risks, both for individual believers and for the church. But the NT reminds us that desperate people take risks, and that God loves to work in and through desperate people (Lk. 1.52-53). Am I desperate for God? Am I willing to take risks to see God's work accomplished in and through me?

4. After noting some of the shifts over the past century in Evangelical approaches to reading the Bible, Menzies suggests that it is time once again to examine the New Testament teaching on tongues. How is Menzies' approach different from that of Evangelicals of a previous generation?

---

[20] Synan, 'Role of Tongues', p. 82.

[21] I also question on theological grounds the trend to move toward dark, 'theater lighting' in our worship services. Does this not minimize the corporate aspect of our worship (the very reason we gather together) and serve to both isolate the individual believer from other worshippers and place an unhealthy emphasis on those leading worship?

PART ONE

LUKE AND TONGUES

Introduction

In the following two chapters, I would like to explore, from Luke's perspective, the role of tongues in the life of the church and the individual believer. I will first highlight the importance of starting our inquiry with the right mindset by describing the assumptions regarding tongues that should inform our study. Then, in Chapter One, I will attempt to elucidate Luke's perspective on tongues, particularly his attitude toward the role of tongues in the church. Then, in Chapter Two, I shall seek to describe Luke's understanding of the role of tongues in the life of the individual believer. Finally, I shall summarize my findings and their significance for contemporary Christians.

Important Assumptions: Tongues or Languages?

Many Christians seeking to examine the biblical teaching on tongues begin with faulty assumptions. Chief among these would be the notion that glossolalia was either non-existent in the early church, or at the most, that it was experienced very rarely by a limited few. The teaching, prevalent in some quarters, that references to 'speaking in tongues' in the NT typically denote the supernatural ability to preach in a foreign language previously unknown to the speaker (xenolalia) has cast a long shadow. Furthermore, the impression is often given that the NT authors rarely discuss this strange practice and that, when they do, they do so with great hesitation and are largely negative and condescending in their remarks. However, a review of the biblical evidence, as we shall see, suggests that these assumptions are flawed and need to be reconsidered.

The phenomenon of speaking in tongues is actually described in numerous passages in the New Testament.[1] In 1 Corinthians 12-14 Paul refers to the gift of tongues (γλώσσαις)[2] and uses the phrase λαλέω γλώσσαις to designate unintelligible utterances inspired by the Spirit.[3] The fact that this gift of tongues refers to unintelligible utterances (e.g. the glossolalia experienced in contemporary Pentecostal churches) rather than known human languages (xenolalia) is confirmed by the fact that Paul explicitly states that these tongues must be interpreted if they are to be understood (1 Cor. 14.6-19, 28; cf. 12.10, 30). Additionally, Paul clearly believes that one can interpret these tongues only if one has a special gift of the Spirit to do so (1 Cor. 12.10). In other words, since Paul does not entertain the possibility that someone with a knowledge of the particular tongue being spoken might be present and thus be able to interpret, it is evident that intelligible human languages are not in view at this point.

In Acts 10.46 and 19.6 Luke also uses the phrase λαλέω γλώσσαις to designate utterances inspired by the Spirit. In Acts 10.46 Peter and his colleagues hear Cornelius and his household 'speaking in tongues and praising God'.[4] Acts 19.6 states that the Ephesian disciples 'spoke in tongues and prophesied'. The literary parallels between the descriptions of speaking in tongues in these passages and 1 Corinthians 12-14 are impressive. All of these texts: (1) associate speaking in tongues with the inspiration of the Holy Spirit; (2) utilize similar vocabulary (λαλέω γλώσσαις); and (3) describe inspired speech associated with worship and prophetic pronouncements. Additionally, since 1 Corinthians 12-14 clearly speaks of unintelligible utterances and there is no indication in either of the

---

[1] There are a total of 35 explicit references to speaking in tongues in the NT. Twenty-eight are found in 1 Corinthians, 23 of these in 1 Corinthians 14. The other occurrences are found in Acts and the Gospel of Mark. See 1 Corinthians 12-14; Acts 2.4-11, 10.46, 19.6; as well as Mk 16.17. For more general references to charismatic activity that probably include speaking in tongues see Rom. 8.26-27; 2 Cor. 5.4; Eph. 5.19, 6.18; Col. 3.16; 1 Thess. 5.19; and Jude 20.

[2] 1 Corinthians 12.10; 12.28; 13.8; 14.22, 26.

[3] 1 Corinthians 12.30; 13.1; 14.2, 4, 6, 13, 18, 23, 27, 39.

[4] All English Scripture citations are taken from the NIV unless otherwise noted. All citations from the Greek NT are from the Nestle-Aland 27th edition. All citations from the LXX are from *Septuaginta*, edited by Alfred Rahlfs, 1979 edition.

Acts passages that known languages are being spoken – indeed, there is no apparent need for a miracle of xenolalia in either instance (what foreign language would they have spoken?) – most English translations, including the NRSV, translate the occurrences of λαλέω γλώσσαις in these texts with reference to speaking in tongues.

The references to 'tongues' (γλώσσαις) in Acts 2.1-13, however, raise interesting questions for those seeking to understand this passage. The first occurrence of γλώσσαις is found in Acts 2.3, where it refers to the visionary 'tongues of fire' that appear and then separate and rest on each of the disciples present. Then, in Acts 2.4 we read that those present were all filled with the Holy Spirit and began to 'speak in other tongues (λαλεῖν ἑτέραις γλώσσαις) as the Spirit enabled them'. This phenomenon creates confusion among the Jews of the crowd who, we are told, represent 'every nation under heaven' (Acts 2.5). The crowd gathered in astonishment because 'each one heard them speaking in his own language' (διαλέκτῳ; Acts 2.6). These details are repeated as Luke narrates the response of the astonished group: 'Are not all these men who are speaking Galileans? Then how is it that each of us hears them in his own native language' (διαλέκτῳ; Acts 2.7-8)? After the crowd lists in amazement the various nations represented by those present, they declare, 'we hear them declaring the wonders of God in our own tongues' (γλώσσαις; Acts 2.11)!

Since Acts 2.11 clearly relates γλώσσαις to the various human languages of those present in the crowd, most scholars interpret the 'tongues' (γλώσσαις) of Acts 2.4 and 2.11 as referring to intelligible speech. The disciples are enabled by the Spirit to declare 'the wonders of God' in human languages that they had not previously learned.[5] This reading of the text has encouraged some translators, including those who produced the NRSV, to translate γλώσσαις in Acts 2.4 and 2.11 with the term 'language' rather than 'tongue'.

While we can understand why translators are tempted to translate the same words in these passages differently – they actually refer to different activities (xenolalia in Acts 2.4 and glossolalia in

---

[5] Although Jenny Everts demonstrates that it is possible to interpret the 'tongues' of Acts 2.4 as referring to glossolalia, the xenolalia reading appears to be the most natural. See Jenny Everts, 'Tongues or Languages? Contextual Consistency in the Translation of Acts 2', *JPT* 4 (1994), pp. 71-80.

Acts 10.46 and 19.6) – this sort of translation creates a real problem. It obscures the fact that Luke uses the same Greek terms to describe what takes place when the Spirit is received in Acts 2.4, Acts 10.46, and Acts 19.6. Why, we may ask, does Luke use the same language to describe each of the events even though they actually refer to different activities? This striking literary connection suggests that Luke has intentionally shaped his narrative in order to highlight this linkage. In other words, the pattern is important to him. Luke *desired* to make the connection: he *desired* to establish Acts 2 as a model.

The significance of the verbal connections between the γλώσσαις (tongues) of these three passages becomes apparent when we examine Luke's understanding of the role of tongues in the life of the church. To this task we now turn.

1

LUKE–ACTS:
TONGUES AND THE CHURCH

Luke–Acts and the Role of Tongues in the Church

We have noted the importance of retaining the verbal connections between the γλώσσαις (tongues) of Acts 2.4, Acts 10.46, and Acts 19.6. The theological significance of these connections should not be missed. The significance of these connections becomes apparent when we examine Luke's understanding of the role of tongues in the life of the church.

Tongues as a Type of Prophecy

A close reading of Luke's narrative reveals that he views speaking in tongues as a special type of prophetic speech. Speaking in tongues is associated with prophecy in each of the three passages which describe this phenomenon in Acts. In Acts 2.17-18 (cf. Acts 2.4) speaking in tongues is specifically described as a fulfillment of Joel's prophecy that in the last days all of God's people will prophesy. The strange sounds of the disciples' tongues-speech, Peter declares, are in fact not the ramblings of drunkards; rather, they represent prophetic utterances issued by God's end-time messengers (Acts 2.13, 15-17). In Acts 19.6 the connection between prophecy and speaking in tongues is again explicitly stated. When Paul laid hands on the Ephesian disciples, the Holy Spirit 'came on them, and they spoke in tongues and prophesied'.

Finally, the association is made again in Acts 10.42-48. In the midst of Peter's sermon to Cornelius and his household, the Holy

Spirit 'came on all those who heard the message' (Acts 10.44). Peter's colleagues 'were astonished that the gift of the Holy Spirit had been poured out even on the Gentiles, for they heard them speaking in tongues and praising God' (Acts 10.45-46). It is instructive to note that the Holy Spirit interrupts Peter just as he has declared, 'He [Jesus] commanded us to preach to the people and to testify that he is the one whom God appointed as judge of the living and the dead. *All the prophets testify about him* that everyone who believes in him receives forgiveness of sins through his name' (Acts 10.42-43).[1] In view of Luke's emphasis on prophetic inspiration throughout his two-volume work and, more specifically, his description of speaking in tongues as prophetic speech in Acts 2.17-18, it can hardly be coincidental that the Holy Spirit breaks in and inspires glossolalia precisely at this point in Peter's sermon. Indeed, as the context makes clear, Peter's colleagues are astonished at what transpires because it testifies to the fact that God has accepted uncircumcised Gentiles. Again, the connection between speaking in tongues and prophecy is crucial for Luke's narrative. In Acts 2.17-18 we are informed that reception of the Spirit of prophecy (i.e. the Pentecostal gift) is the exclusive privilege of 'the servants' of God and that it typically results in miraculous and audible speech.[2] Speaking in tongues is presented as one manifestation of this miraculous, Spirit-inspired speech (Acts 2.4, 17-18). So, when Cornelius and his household burst forth in tongues, this act provides demonstrative proof that they are in fact part of the end-time prophetic band of which Joel prophesied. They too are connected to the prophets that 'testify' about Jesus (Acts 10.43). This astonishes Peter's colleagues, because they recognize the clear implications that flow from this dramatic event: since Cornelius and his household are prophets, they must also be 'servants' of the Lord (that is, members of the people of God). How, then, can Peter and the others withhold baptism from them (Acts 10.47-48)?

---

[1] Italics mine.

[2] Of the eight instances where Luke describes the initial reception of the Spirit by a person or group, five specifically allude to some form of inspired speech as an immediate result (Lk. 1.41-42; 1.67; Acts 2.4; 10.46; 19.6) and one implies the occurrence of such activity (Acts 8.15, 18). In the remaining two instances, although inspired speech is absent from Luke's account (Lk. 3.22; Acts 9.17), it is a prominent feature in the pericopes that follow (Lk. 4.14, 18-19; Acts 9.20).

The importance of this connection in the narrative is highlighted further in Acts 11.15-18. Here, as Peter recounts the events associated with the conversion of Cornelius and his household, he emphasizes that 'the Holy Spirit came on them as he had come on us at the beginning' (Acts 11.15) and then declares, 'God gave them the same gift as he gave us …' (Acts 11.17). The fact that Jewish disciples at Pentecost and Gentile believers at Caesarea all spoke in tongues is not incidental to Luke's purposes; rather, it represents a significant theme in his story of the movement of the gospel from Jews in Jerusalem to Gentiles in Rome and beyond.

[handwritten margin note: Good Cornelius]

Salvation History and Tongues in Luke–Acts

Some might be tempted to suggest at this point that the special role that speaking in tongues plays as a sign in Acts 2 and Acts 10 indicates that, in Luke's view, this phenomenon was limited to these historically significant events in the early days of the founding of the church. This, however, would be to misread Luke's narrative. Luke states the point with particular clarity in Acts 2.17-21:

[v. 17] *In the last days, God says,* [Joel: 'after these things']
I will pour out my Spirit on all people.
Your sons and daughters will prophesy
Your young men will see visions, [Joel: these lines are inverted]
Your old men will dream dreams.
[v. 18] *Even* on *my* servants, both men and women, [additions to Joel]
I will pour out my Spirit in those days,
And they will prophesy.
[v. 19] I will show wonders in the heaven *above*
And *signs* on the earth *below*,
Blood and fire and billows of smoke.
[v. 20] The sun will be turned to darkness and the moon to blood
Before the coming of the great and glorious day of the Lord.
[v. 21] And everyone who calls on the name of the Lord will be saved.[3]

---

[3] Acts 2.17-21; the key modifications of Joel 2.28-32 are italicized.

We should remember that here Luke carefully shapes this quotation from the LXX in order to highlight important theological themes and truths. Three modifications are particularly striking.

First, in v. 17 Luke alters the order of the two lines that refer to young men having visions and old men dreaming dreams. In Joel, the old men dreaming dreams comes first. But Luke reverses the order: 'Your young men will see visions, your old men will dream dreams' (Acts 2.17). Luke gives the reference to 'visions' pride of place in order to highlight a theme that he sees as vitally important and which recurs throughout his narrative. Although words associated with 'dreams' are rare in Luke–Acts,[4] Luke loves to recount stories in which God directs his church through visions.[5] The visions of Paul and Ananias (Acts 9.10-11), of Peter and Cornelius (Acts 10.3, 17), Paul's Macedonian vision (Acts 16.9-10), and his vision at Corinth (Acts 18.9-10) are but a few. Luke is not fixated on visions; rather, he seeks to encourage his readers to embrace an important truth. God delights to lead us, his end-time prophets, in very personal and special ways, including visions, angelic visitations, and the prompting of the Spirit, so that we might fulfill our calling to take the gospel to 'the ends of the earth'.

Secondly, Luke inserts the phrase, 'And they will prophesy', into the quotation in v. 18. It is as if Luke is saying, 'whatever you do, don't miss this!' In these last days the servants of God will be anointed by the Spirit to proclaim his good news and declare his praises. They will prophesy! This is what is *now* taking place. The speaking in tongues that you hear, declares Peter, is a fulfillment of Joel's prophecy. This special form of Spirit-inspired prophetic speech serves as a unique sign that 'the last days' have arrived (cf.

---

[4] The term translated 'shall dream' is a future passive of ἐνυπνιάζομαι. This verb occurs only in Acts 2.17 and in Jude 8 in the entire New Testament. The noun, ἐνύπνιον ('dream'), is found nowhere else in Acts or the rest of the New Testament.

[5] The noun translated 'visions' in v. 17, ὅρασις, occurs four times in the New Testament and only here in Acts. The other three occurrences are all found in Revelation. However, Luke uses another term, a close cousin to ὅρασις, the neuter noun, ὅραμα, often and at decisive points in his narrative to refer to 'visions'. The noun ὅραμα occurs 12 times in the New Testament and 11 of these occurrences are found in the book of Acts (Acts 7.31; 9.10, 12; 10. 3, 17, 19; 11.5; 12.9; 16.9, 10; 18.9; and then also in Mt. 17.9).

Acts 2.33-36; 10.45-46). Of course, this theme of Spirit-inspired witness runs throughout the narrative of Acts.[6]

Thirdly, with the addition of a few words in v. 19, Luke transforms Joel's text to read: 'I will show wonders in the heaven *above*, and *signs* on the earth *below*'. The significance of these insertions, which form a collocation of 'wonders' and 'signs', becomes apparent when we look at the larger context of Acts. The first verse that follows the Joel citation declares, 'Jesus ... was a man accredited by God to you by miracles, *wonders and signs*' (Acts 2.22). And throughout the book of Acts we read of the followers of Jesus working 'wonders and signs'.[7] In this way, Luke links the miraculous events associated with Jesus (Acts 2.22) and his disciples (e.g. Acts 2.43) together with the cosmic portents listed by Joel (see Acts 2.19b-20) as 'signs and wonders' that mark the era of fulfillment, 'the last days'. For Luke, 'these last days' – that period inaugurated with Jesus' birth and leading up to the Day of the Lord – represents an epoch marked by 'signs and wonders'. According to Luke, then, visions, prophecy, and miracles – all of these should characterize the life of the church in these last days. Acts 2.17-21 indicates that Luke is conscious of the significant role that these phenomena have played in the growth of the early church and that he anticipates these activities will continue to characterize the ministry of the church in these 'last days'.

This conclusion, of course, has a direct bearing on the question at hand, on how we should view tongues today. As a manifestation of prophecy, Luke suggests that tongues have an ongoing role to play in the life of the church. Remember, a characteristic of 'the last days' – that era of fulfillment that begins with the birth of Jesus and ends with his second coming – is that all of God's people will prophesy (Acts 2.17-18). The fact that Luke recounts various instances of the fulfillment of this prophecy that feature speaking in tongues encourages the reader to understand that, like 'signs and wonders' and bold, Spirit-inspired witness for Jesus, speaking in tongues will characterize the life of the church in these last days. To

---

[6] See especially Acts 4.13, 31; 5.32; 6.10; 9.31; 13.9, 52.

[7] Nine of the 16 occurrences of 'signs and wonders' in the NT are found in Acts: Acts 2.19, 22, 43; 4.30; 5.12; 6.8; 7.36; 14.3; 15.12.

suggest otherwise runs counter to Luke's explicitly stated message, not to mention that of Paul (1 Cor. 14.39).

Jesus Our Model

Luke not only views speaking in tongues as a special type of prophetic speech that has an ongoing role in the life of the church, there are also indications that he sees this form of exuberant, inspired speech modeled in the life of Jesus. Apart from the general parallels between Jesus and his disciples with reference to Spirit-inspired prophetic speech (e.g. Lk. 4.18-19; Acts 2.17-18), there is a more specific parallel found in Lk. 10.21, a text unique to Luke. 'At that time Jesus, full of joy through the Holy Spirit, said, "I praise you, Father, Lord of heaven and earth ...'"

Luke provides an interesting context for this joyful outburst of thanksgiving. It occurs in response to the return of the Seventy from their mission. As we have noted elsewhere, the sending of the Seventy (Lk. 10.1, 17) echoes the prophetic anointing of the seventy elders in Numbers 11.[8] Some scholars, such as Gordon Wenham, describe the prophesying narrated in Num. 11.24-30 as an instance of 'unintelligible ecstatic utterance, what the New Testament terms speaking in tongues'.[9]

On the heels of this passage, Luke describes Jesus' inspired exultation. Particularly important for our discussion is the manner in which Luke introduces Jesus' words of praise: 'he rejoiced in the Holy Spirit and said' (ἠγαλλιάσατο ἐν τῷ πνεύματι τῷ ἁγίῳ καὶ εἶπεν; Lk. 10.21).[10] The verb, ἀγαλλιάω (rejoice), employed here by Luke, is used frequently in the LXX. It is usually found in the Psalms and the poetic portions of the Prophets, and it denotes spiritual exultation that issues forth in praise to God for his mighty acts.[11] The subject of the verb is not simply ushered into a state of

[8] See also Robert P. Menzies, 'The Sending of the Seventy and Luke's Purpose', in Paul Alexander, Jordan D. May, and Robert Reid (eds.), *Trajectories in the Book of Acts: Essays in Honor of John Wesley Wyckoff* (Eugene, OR: Wipf & Stock, 2010), pp. 87-113.

[9] Gordon Wenham, *Numbers: An Introduction and Commentary* (Downers Grove, IL: Inter-Varsity Press, 1981), p. 109. I am indebted to my good friend, Grant Hochman, for pointing me to this reference.

[10] I am following the *American Standard Version* here for the English translation.

[11] R. Bultmann, 'ἀγαλλιάομαι', TDNT, I, p. 19; W.G. Morrice, *Joy in the New Testament* (Exeter: Paternoster Press, 1984), p. 20.

sacred rapture; he also 'declares the acts of God'.[12] In the New Testament the verb is used in a similar manner. The linkage between ἀγαλλιάω and the declaration of the mighty acts of God is particularly striking in Luke–Acts.[13] The verb describes the joyful praise of Mary (Lk. 1.47), Jesus (Lk. 10.21), and David (Acts 2.26) in response to God's salvific activity in Jesus. In Lk. 1.47 and 10.21 the verb is specifically linked to the inspiration of the Holy Spirit and in Acts 2.25-30 David is described as a prophet. This verb, then, was for Luke a particularly appropriate way of describing prophetic activity.

The reference in Acts 2.26 is especially interesting; for here, the verb ἀγαλλιάω is associated with the word γλῶσσα (tongue). In a quotation from Ps. 16.9 (Ps. 15.9, LXX), Peter cites David as saying, 'Therefore my heart is glad and my tongue rejoices (καὶ ἠγαλλιάσατο ἡ γλῶσσά μου) …' This association of ἀγαλλιάω with γλῶσσα should not surprise us, for five of the eight references to γλῶσσα in Luke–Acts describe experiences of spiritual exultation that result in praise.[14] All of this indicates that, for Luke, ἀγαλλιάω and γλῶσσα, when associated with the inspiration of the Holy Spirit, are terms that describe special instances of prophetic inspiration, instances in which a person or group experiences spiritual exultation and, as a result, bursts forth in praise.

We conclude that Lk. 10.21 describes Jesus' prayer of thanksgiving in terms reminiscent of speaking in tongues: inspired by the Spirit, Jesus bursts forth in exuberant and joyful praise. Although it is quite possible that Luke's readers would have understood this outburst of inspired praise to include unintelligible utterances (i.e. glossolalia), at this point we are unable to offer little more than conjecture. However, we will return to this question and examine it in more detail in Chapter Three. For now we can only offer a guarded conclusion: the account describes an experience that is very much like that of speaking in tongues, an experience of spiritual rapture that produces joyful praise. What is abundantly clear is that Luke presents Jesus' Spirit-inspired prophetic ministry, including his bold

---

[12] Bultmann, 'ἀγαλλιάομαι', p. 20.

[13] The linkage is made explicit in three out of four occurrences of the verb (Lk. 1.47; 10.21; Acts 2.26). The only exception is Acts 16.34.

[14] These five include: Lk. 1.64, Acts 2.4, 2.26, 10.46, 19.6. The other three references to γλῶσσα are found in Lk. 16.24; Acts 2.3, 11.

proclamation and exultant praise, as a model for his readers,[15] living as they do, in these 'last days'.

Conclusion

We may summarize our argument to this point as follows:

1. Glossolalia was well known and widely practiced in the early church. Luke's references to speaking in tongues (λαλέω γλώσσαις) in Acts 10.46, 19.6, and possibly (but not likely) 2.4, designate unintelligible utterances inspired by the Spirit rather than the speaking of human languages previously not learned. However we interpret this latter text (Acts 2.4), the importance of the verbal connections between the λαλέω γλώσσαις (to speak in tongues) of Acts 2.4, Acts 10.46, and Acts 19.6 should not be missed.

2. Luke's narrative reveals that he views speaking in tongues as a special type of prophetic speech. Speaking in tongues is associated with prophecy in each of the three passages which describe this phenomenon in Acts (Acts 2.4; 10.46; 19.6).

3. As a special manifestation of prophecy, Luke indicates that glossolalia has an ongoing role to play in the life of the church. This is evident from Luke's modification of Joel's prophecy in Acts 2.17-21. Here, we see that tongues serve as a sign of the arrival of the last days (Acts 2.17-21) and also of Jesus' resurrection and Lordship (Acts 2.33-36). Tongues, it should be noted, continue to serve as a demonstrable sign of reception of the prophetic gift throughout Luke's narrative (Acts 10.44-48; 19.6-7). This text (Acts 2.17-21), particularly as it is seen in the larger context of Luke–Acts, also establishes that, in Luke's perspective, speaking in tongues will continue to characterize the life of the church in these last days (that is, until Jesus returns).

4. Luke presents Jesus' experience of the Spirit and his life of prayer as important models for his readers. Luke 10.21, which describes Jesus, in language reminiscent of speaking in tongues,

---

[15] Luke's emphasis on prayer, and particularly the prayers and prayer-life of Jesus, is widely recognized by contemporary scholars. Luke also associates prayer with the Holy Spirit in a unique way (e.g. Lk. 3.21-22; 11.13; Acts 4.31).

bursting forth with Spirit-inspired, exuberant and joyful praise, is no exception.

Application

A single lady, Mattie Ledbetter was ordained a missionary to South China in 1911. She served for many years in Fat Shan (modern day Foshan in Guangdong Province), establishing two outstations and serving in an orphanage. A church she planted in Fat Shan still exists today. Mattie often traveled by horseback from village to village distributing Bibles and preaching. In a letter dated Nov. 30, 1920 she offers a vivid picture of her prayer life. She writes,

> Once recently at morning prayer ... I sunk on the floor under the power of God and lay there three hours. Every little while the power would shake me from head to foot and the Lord would give me a prayer or a song or reveal something to me ... and Oh how sweetly Jesus spoke to my soul. I was melted in love.[16]

In 1928 Mattie, suffering from exhaustion, traveled to Hong Kong for a time of rest and recuperation. Little did she know that God would use her to preach evangelistic crusades in a tent and in this way pioneer a vibrant church in Hong Kong. Hong Kong First Assembly of God now numbers close to 1,000 believers. Mattie died of dysentery in Hong Kong on March 2, 1938 at the age of 67.[17]

I am moved by Mattie's story because it shows the incredible impact that one person can have when led and empowered by the Holy Spirit. It also reveals the true source of Mattie's amazing strength and courage: times of fervent prayer that nurtured intimate relationship with Jesus. Out of these rich experiences flowed direction, inspiration, and power. For Mattie these wonderful experiences were often marked by speaking in tongues.

Mattie's story raises some challenging but also inspiring questions for me. Do I make time for this kind of deep, intimate prayer life? Do I follow the example of Jesus and make room for those

---

[16] Nov. 30, 1920 letter from AG Archives.
[17] *The Pentecostal Evangel* (March 26, 1938), p. 7.

special moments of communion with God when I am caught up in spiritual rapture and burst forth in praise?

Reflection Questions

1. Luke uses essentially the same language to describe the disciples' experience of speaking in tongues in Acts 2.4, 10.46, and 19.6. This is the case, even though Acts 2 probably describes xenolalia and Acts 10 and 19 speak of glossolalia. What does this suggest about Luke's purpose?

2. Luke presents tongues as a special type of prophetic speech. What might this mean for me and for my church? When I speak in tongues, what symbolic message is being conveyed to my fellow Christians and to me?

3. Some feel that the gift of tongues was given only to the apostles. It was given as a sign to enable and validate their testimony about Jesus. How does Peter's sermon, especially his quotation from Joel 2 (Acts 2.17-21), refute this argument?

4. Some also ask, if God intended for us to speak in tongues, why didn't Jesus do so? How does Menzies answer this question? What sort of model does Jesus provide (Lk. 10.21)?

2

Luke–Acts:
Tongues and the Believer

In the previous chapter we have seen that Luke provides an impressive resume for tongues. However, an important question still remains unanswered. Does Luke envision every believer actively engaging in glossolalia? Put another way, according to Luke, is speaking in tongues available to all? In my previous writings, I suggested that Luke does not consciously address this question. I went on to argue, however, that Paul does; and that he does so in the affirmative.[1] Nevertheless, I now believe that my judgment concerning Luke was a bit hasty. There are several texts in Luke's gospel, all unique to Luke or uniquely shaped by him, that reveal a clear intent to encourage his readers to pray for prophetic anointings, experiences that will inevitably produce bold witness and joyful praise. Luke's narrative calls for his readers to recognize that these pneumatic anointings, these experiences of spiritual rapture which issue forth in praise, are indeed available to every disciple of Jesus and that they will routinely take the form of glossolalia. To these key texts we now turn.

Luke 19.39-40

We begin our examination of Luke's understanding of the role of tongues in the life of the believer by considering Luke's account of

---

[1] See Menzies, *Spirit and Power*, pp. 121-32.

Jesus' triumphal entry into Jerusalem (Lk. 19.28-44). It is a story found in various forms in all four gospels. It is widely recognized that Luke closely follows Mark's account (Mk 11.1-10), but with one significant exception. Luke 19.39-40 is found only in Luke's gospel.

> Some of the Pharisees in the crowd said to Jesus, 'Teacher, rebuke your disciples!'

> 'I tell you', he replied, 'if they keep quiet, the stones will cry out' (Lk. 19.39-40).

At first glance the inclusion of this material in this story may not appear striking. However, when viewed in the light of Luke's emphasis on Spirit-inspired praise and witness throughout Luke–Acts, it takes on special meaning. Luke's narrative is filled with the praises of God's people, all of whom declare the mighty deeds of God. The chorus of praise begins in the infancy narratives with Elizabeth's Blessing (Lk. 1.42-45), Mary's Magnificat (Lk. 1.46-55), Zechariah's Song (Lk. 1.67-79), and Simeon's Prophecy (Lk. 2.29-35). Angels join in as well (Lk. 2.13-14). The sound of Spirit-inspired praise continues with Jesus' joyful outburst (Lk. 10.21-24). The angelic praise of Lk. 2.13-14 is then echoed by the crowd of disciples as they welcome Jesus as he enters into Jerusalem (Lk. 19.37-38). Of course in Lk. 19.39-40 Luke uniquely highlights the significance of this praise. The chorus is again picked up on the day of Pentecost with the dramatic declaration of God's mighty deeds by those who have been filled with the Holy Spirit (Acts 2.1-13). It continues throughout Luke's narrative in the form of bold, Spirit-inspired witness to Jesus.[2] Irruptions of prophecy and praise are again associated with the Spirit and glossolalia in Acts 10.46 and Acts 19.6.

These texts, collectively, constitute a motif that is clearly close to Luke's heart. In these last days, Luke declares, the Spirit will inspire his end-time prophets to declare God's mighty deeds, chief of which is the resurrection of Jesus. Indeed, if the disciples remain silent, 'the stones will cry out!' The message to Luke's church, a church facing opposition and persecution,[3] could hardly be missed.

---

[2] See, for example, Acts 4.13, 31; 5.32; 6.10; 9.31; 13.9, 52.

[3] On Luke's church as a community facing persecution, see my essay in Max Turner's *Festschrift*: Robert Menzies, 'The Persecuted Prophets: A Mirror-Image

Praise and bold witness go hand in hand, they are both the necessary and inevitable consequence of being filled with the Holy Spirit.

Luke 10.1-16

Let us now turn to another text unique to Luke's gospel, Luke's account of the Sending of the Seventy (Lk. 10.1-16). All three synoptic gospels record Jesus' words of instruction to the Twelve as he sends them out on their mission. However, only Luke records a second, larger sending of disciples (Lk. 10.1-16). In Lk. 10.1 we read, 'After this the Lord appointed seventy-two [some mss read, 'seventy'] others and sent them two by two ahead of him to every town and place where he was about to go'. A series of detailed instructions follow. Finally, Jesus reminds them of their authority, 'He who listens to you listens to me; he who rejects you rejects me; but he who rejects me rejects him who sent me' (10.16).

A central question centers on the number of disciples that Jesus sent out and its significance. The manuscript evidence is, at this point, divided. Some manuscripts read 'seventy', while others list the number as 'seventy-two'. Bruce Metzger, in his article on this question, noted that the external manuscript evidence is evenly divided and internal considerations are also inconclusive. Metzger thus concluded that the number 'cannot be determined with confidence'.[4] More recent scholarship has largely agreed with Metzger, with a majority opting cautiously for the authenticity of 'seventy-two' as the more difficult reading.[5] Although we cannot determine

---

of Luke's Spirit-Inspired Church', in I. Howard Marshall, Volker Rabens, and Cornelis Bennema (eds.), *The Spirit and Christ in the New Testament & Christian Theology* (Grand Rapids: Eerdmans, 2012), pp. 52-70.

[4] Bruce Metzger, 'Seventy or Seventy-Two Disciples?', *NTS* 5 (1959), pp. 299-306 (quote, p. 306). See also the response of Sidney Jellicoe, 'St Luke and the "Seventy (-Two)"', *NTS* 6 (1960), pp. 319-21.

[5] All of the following scholars favor the 'seventy-two' reading as original: Darrell L. Bock, *Luke 9.51-24.53* (Baker Exegetical Commentary of the New Testament; Grand Rapids: Baker Academic, 1996), p. 994; I. Howard Marshall, *The Gospel of Luke: A Commentary on the Greek Text* (NIGCT; Grand Rapids: Eerdmans, 1978), p. 415; Joel Green, *The Gospel of Luke* (NICNT; Grand Rapids: Eerdmans, 1997), p. 409; Robert C. Tannehill, *The Narrative Unity of Luke–Acts: A Literary Interpretation, Volume 1. The Gospel According to Luke* (Philadelphia: Fortress Press, 1986), p. 233; Craig Evans, *Luke* (New International Biblical Commentary; Peabody: Hendrickson, 1990), p. 172. One exception to this general rule is John Nol-

the number with confidence, it will be important to keep the divided nature of the manuscript evidence in mind as we wrestle with the significance of this text.

Most scholars agree that the number (for convenience, we will call it 'seventy') has symbolic significance. Certainly Jesus' selection of twelve disciples was no accident. The number twelve clearly symbolizes the reconstitution of Israel (Gen. 35.23-26), the people of God. This suggests that the number seventy is rooted in the OT narrative and has symbolic significance as well. A number of proposals have been put forward,[6] but I would argue that the background for the reference to the 'seventy' is to be found in Num. 11.24-30. This passage describes how the Lord 'took of the Spirit that was on [Moses] and put the Spirit on the seventy elders' (Num. 11.25). This resulted in the seventy elders, who had gathered around the Tent, prophesying for a short duration. However, two other elders, Eldad and Medad, did not go to the Tent; rather, they remained in the camp. But the Spirit also fell on them and they too began to prophesy and continued to do so. Joshua, hearing this news, rushed to Moses and urged him to stop them. Moses replied, 'Are you jealous for my sake? I wish that all the Lord's people were prophets and that the Lord would put his Spirit on them!' (Num. 11.29).

The Numbers 11 proposal has a number of significant advantages over other explanations: (1) it accounts for the two textual traditions underlying Luke 10.1 (How many actually prophesied in Numbers 11?); (2) it finds explicit fulfillment in the narrative of Acts; (3) it ties into one of the great themes of Luke–Acts, the work of the Holy Spirit; and (4) numerous allusions to Moses and his actions in Luke's travel narrative support our suggestion that the symbolism for Luke's reference to the Seventy should be found in Numbers 11.[7]

---

land, who favors the 'seventy' reading (Nolland, *Luke 9.21-18.34* [Word Biblical Commentary 35B; Dallas, TX: Word, 1993], p. 546).

[6] For the various options see Metzger, 'Seventy or Seventy-Two Disciples', pp. 303-304 and Bock, *Luke 9.51-24.53*, p. 1015.

[7] For more detailed support of this position, see Robert P. Menzies, *The Language of the Spirit: Interpreting and Translating Charismatic Terms* (Cleveland, TN: CPT Press, 2010), pp. 73-82.

With this background in mind, the significance of the symbolism is found in the expansion of the number of disciples 'sent out' into mission from the Twelve to the Seventy. The reference to the Seventy evokes memories of Moses' wish that 'all the Lord's people were prophets', and, in this way, points ahead to Pentecost (Acts 2), where this wish is initially and dramatically fulfilled. This wish continues to be fulfilled throughout Acts as Luke describes the coming of the empowering Spirit of prophecy to other new centers of missionary activity, such as those gathered together in Samaria (Acts 8.14-17), Cornelius' house (Acts 10.44-48), and Ephesus (Acts 19.1-7). The reference to the Seventy, then, does not simply anticipate the mission of the church to the Gentiles; rather, it foreshadows the outpouring of the Spirit on all the servants of the Lord and their universal participation in the mission of God (Acts 2.17-18; cf. 4.31).[8] In Luke's view, every member of the church is called (Luke 24.45-49; Acts 1.4-8/Isa. 49.6) and empowered (Acts 2.17-21; cf. 4.31) to be a prophet. Luke 10.1 anticipates the fulfillment of this reality.

It is important to note that the ecstatic speech of the elders in Numbers 11 constitutes the backdrop against which Luke interprets the Pentecostal and subsequent outpourings of the Spirit. It would appear that Luke views every believer as (at least potentially) an end-time prophet, and that he anticipates that they too will issue forth in Spirit-inspired ecstatic speech.[9] This is the clear implication of his narrative, which includes repetitive fulfillments of Moses' wish that reference glossolalia.

Of the four instances in the book of Acts where Luke actually describes the initial coming of the Spirit, three explicitly cite glossolalia as the immediate result (Acts 2.4; 10.46; 19.6) and the other one (Acts 8.14-19) strongly implies it.[10] This is the case even though

---

[8] Keith F. Nickle, *Preaching the Gospel of Luke: Proclaiming God's Royal Rule* (Louisville: Westminster John Knox Press, 2000), p. 117: 'The "Seventy" is the church in its entirety, including Luke's own community, announcing the in-breaking of God's royal rule throughout the length and breadth of God's creation'.

[9] With the term, 'ecstatic', I mean 'pertaining to or flowing from an experience of intense joy'. I do not wish to imply a loss of control with this term. While glossolalia transcends our reasoning faculties, the experience does not render them useless (cf. 1 Cor. 14.28, 32-33).

[10] Paul's experience of the Spirit is not actually described (Acts 9.17-19); rather, it is implied.

Luke could have easily used other language, particularly in Acts 2, to describe what had transpired. The Acts 8 passage has various purposes. However, when it is viewed in the context of Luke's larger narrative, there can be little doubt in the reader's mind concerning the cause of Simon's ill-fated attempt to purchase the ability to dispense the Spirit. The motif is transparent; Luke's point is made: the Pentecostal gift, as a fulfillment of Moses' wish (Num. 11.29) and Joel's prophecy (Joel 2.28-32), is a prophetic anointing that enables its recipient to bear bold witness for Jesus and, this being the case, it is marked by the ecstatic speech characteristic of prophets (i.e. glossolalia).

This explains why Luke considered tongues to be a sign of the reception of the Pentecostal gift. Certainly Luke does present tongues as evidence of the Spirit's coming. On the day of Pentecost Peter declares that the tongues of the disciples served as a sign. Their tongues not only established the fact that they, the disciples of Jesus, were the end-time prophets of which Joel prophesied; their tongues also marked the arrival of the last days (Acts 2.17-21) and served to establish the fact that Jesus had risen from the dead and is Lord (Acts 2.33-36). In Acts 10.44-48 'speaking in tongues' is again 'depicted as proof positive and sufficient to convince Peter's companions' that the Spirit had been poured out on the Gentiles.[11] In Acts 19.6 tongues and prophecy are cited as the immediate results of the coming of the Spirit, the incontrovertible evidence of an affirmative answer to Paul's question posed earlier in the narrative: 'Did you receive the Holy Spirit when you believed?'

It is interesting to note that Luke does not share the angst of many modern Christians concerning the possibility of false tongues. Luke does not offer guidelines for discerning whether tongues are genuine or fake, from God or from some other source.[12] Rather, Luke assumes that the Christian community will know and experi-

---

[11] James D.G. Dunn, *Jesus and the Spirit: A Study of the Religious and Charismatic Experience of Jesus and the First Christians as Reflected in the New Testament* (Philadelphia: Westminster Press, 1975), p. 189.

[12] This sort of lacuna led James Dunn, over thirty years ago, to describe Luke's perspective as 'lop-sided' (Dunn, *Jesus and the Spirit*, pp. 191, 195). Given the dramatic rise of the Pentecostal movement and the sad state of many traditional churches, one wonders if Professor Dunn might now be more sympathetic to Luke's enthusiastic approach. Perhaps by listening more carefully to Luke the church can regain its balance.

ence that which is needed and good. This observation leads us to our next text.

Luke 11.9-13

Another text that reflects Luke's desire to encourage his church to experience the prophetic inspiration of the Spirit and all that entails (i.e. joyful praise, glossolalia, and bold witness) is found in Lk. 11.13. This verse, which forms the climax to Jesus' teaching on prayer, again testifies to the fact that Luke views the work of the Holy Spirit described in Acts as relevant for the life of his church. Luke is not writing wistfully about an era of charismatic activity in the distant past.[13] Luke 11.13 reads, 'If you then, though you are evil, know how to give good gifts to your children, how much more will your Father in heaven give the Holy Spirit to those who ask Him!' It is instructive to note that the parallel passage in Matthew's gospel contains slightly different phrasing: 'how much more will your Father in heaven give *good gifts* to those who ask Him!' (Mt. 7.11).[14] It is virtually certain that Luke has interpreted the 'good gifts' in his source material with a reference to the 'Holy Spirit'.[15] Luke, then, provides us with a Spirit-inspired, authoritative commentary on this saying of Jesus. Three important implications follow.

First, Luke's alteration of the Matthean (or Q) form of the saying anticipates the post-resurrection experience of the church.[16] This is evident from the fact that the promise that the Father will give the Holy Spirit to those who ask begins to be realized only at Pentecost. By contemporizing the text in this way, Luke stresses the relevance

---

[13] Contra the judgment of Hans Conzelmann, *Acts of the Apostles* (Philadelphia: Fortress Press, 1987 [German original, 1963]), pp. 15, 159-60.

[14] Italics are mine.

[15] Reasons for this conclusion include: (1) the fact that the reference to the Holy Spirit breaks the parallelism of the 'good gifts' given by earthly fathers and 'the good gifts' given by our heavenly Father; (2) Luke often inserts references to the Holy Spirit into his source material; (3) Matthew never omits or adds references to the Holy Spirit in his sources.

[16] J. Fitzmyer, *The Gospel According to Luke*, *Vol. 2* (AB 28; New York: Doubleday, 1985), p. 916; E.E. Ellis, *The Gospel of Luke* (NCB; London: Oliphants, Marshall, Morgan, & Scott, 1974), p. 164; R. Stronstad, *The Charismatic Theology of St. Luke* (Peabody, MA: Hendrickson, 1984), p. 46.

of the saying for the post-Pentecostal community to which he writes. It would seem that for Luke there is no neat line of separation dividing the apostolic church from his church or ours. Quite the contrary, Luke calls his readers to follow in their footsteps.

Second, the context indicates that the promise is made to disciples (Lk. 11.1). Thus, Luke's contemporized version of the saying is clearly directed to the members of the Christian community.[17] Since it is addressed to Christians, the promise cannot refer to an initiatory or soteriological gift.[18] This judgment finds confirmation in the repetitive character of the exhortations to pray in Lk. 11.9:[19] prayer for the Spirit (and, in light of the promise, we may presume this includes the reception of the Spirit) is to be an ongoing practice. The gift of the Holy Spirit to which Luke refers neither initiates one into the new age, nor is it to be received only once;[20] rather, this pneumatic gift is given to disciples and it is to be experienced on an ongoing basis.

Third, Luke's usage elsewhere indicates that he viewed the gift of the Holy Spirit in 11.13 as a prophetic enabling. On two occasions in Luke–Acts the Spirit is given to those praying;[21] in both the Spirit is portrayed as the source of prophetic activity. Luke's account of Jesus' baptism indicates that Jesus received the Spirit after his baptism while praying (Lk. 3.21). This gift of the Spirit, portrayed principally as the source of prophetic power (Lk. 4.18-19), equipped Jesus for his messianic task. Later, in Acts 4.31 the disciples, after

---

[17] The scholarly consensus affirms that Luke–Acts was addressed primarily to Christians.

[18] G.T. Montague, *The Holy Spirit: Growth of a Biblical Tradition* (New York: Paulist Press, 1976), pp. 259-60.

[19] Note the repetitive or continuous action implicit in the verbs in Lk. 11.9: αἰτεῖτε (ask), ζητεῖτε (seek), κρούετε (knock).

[20] F. Büchsel notes the repetitive character of the exhortation (*Der Geist Gottes im Neuen Testament* [Gütersloh: C. Bertlesmann, 1926], pp. 189-90). So also Montague, *Spirit*, pp. 259-60.

[21] Acts 8.15, 17 represents the only instance in Luke–Acts, apart from the two texts discussed above, where reception of the Spirit is explicitly associated with prayer. However here the Spirit is bestowed on the Samaritans in response to the prayer of Peter and John. While the situation in Acts 8.15, 17 is not a true parallel to Lk. 11.13, in Acts 8.15, 17 the Spirit is also portrayed in prophetic terms. Prayer is implicitly associated with the reception of the Spirit at Pentecost (Acts 1.14; 2.4). Here also the gift of the Spirit is presented as a prophetic endowment. So also Acts 9.17, though here the actual reception of the Spirit is not described.

having prayed, 'were all filled with the Holy Spirit and spoke the word of God boldly'. Again the Spirit given in response to prayer is the impetus for prophetic activity.

What sort of prophetic activity did Luke anticipate would accompany this bestowal of the Spirit? Certainly a reading of Luke's narrative would suggest a wide range of possibilities: joyful praise, glossolalia, visions, bold witness in the face of persecution, to name a few. However, several aspects of Luke's narrative suggest that glossolalia was one of the expected outcomes in Luke's mind and in the minds of his readers.

First, as we noted, Luke's narrative suggests that glossolalia typically accompanies the initial reception of the Spirit. Furthermore, Luke highlights the fact that glossolalia serves as an external sign of the prophetic gift. These elements of Luke's account would undoubtedly encourage readers in Luke's church, like they have with contemporary readers, to seek the prophetic gift, *complete with its accompanying external sign*. In short, in Lk. 11.13 Luke encourages his church to pray for an experience of spiritual rapture that will produce power and praise in their lives, an experience similar to those modeled by Jesus (Lk. 3.21-22; 10.21) and the early church (Acts 2.4; 10.46; 19.6). The reader would naturally assume glossolalia to be a normal, frequent, and expected part of this experience.

Second, in view of the emphasis in this passage on asking (v. 9) and the Father's willingness to respond (v. 13), it would seem natural for Luke's readers to ask a question that again is often asked by contemporary Christians, how will we know when we have received this gift? Here we hear echoes of Paul's question in Acts 19.2. Of course, Luke has provided a clear answer. The arrival of prophetic power has a visible, external sign: glossolalia. This is not to say that there are not other ways in which the Spirit's power and presence are made known to us. This is simply to affirm that Luke's narrative indicates that a visible, external sign does exist and that he and his readers would naturally expect to manifest this sign.

I would add that this sign must have been tremendously encouraging for Luke's church as it is for countless contemporary Christians. It signified their connection with the apostolic church and confirmed their identity as end-time prophets. I find it interesting that so many believers from traditional churches today react negatively to the notion of glossolalia as a visible sign. They often ask, should we really emphasize a visible sign like tongues? Yet these same Christians participate in a liturgical form of worship that is filled with sacraments and imagery; a form of worship that emphasizes visible signs. Signs are valuable when they point to something significant. Luke and his church clearly understood this.

Finally, the question should be asked, why would Luke need to encourage his readers not to be afraid of receiving a bad or harmful gift (note the snake and scorpion of vv. 11-12)?[22] Why would he need to encourage his church to pursue this gift of the Spirit? If the gift is quiet, internal, and ethereal, why would there be any concern? However, if the gift includes glossolalia, which is noisy, unintelligible, and has many pagan counterparts,[23] then the concerns make sense.[24] Luke's response is designed to quell any fears. The Father gives good gifts. We need not fret or fear.

In short, through his skillful editing of this saying of Jesus (Luke 11.13), Luke encourages post-Pentecostal disciples to pray for a prophetic anointing, an experience of spiritual rapture that will produce power and praise in their lives, an experience similar to those modeled by Jesus (Lk. 3.21-22; 10.21) and the early church (Acts 2.4; 10.46; 19.6). The reader would naturally expect glossolalia to be a normal, frequent, and expected part of this experience. The fact that Luke viewed glossolalia as a significant component of this bestowal of the Spirit is suggested by the larger context of Luke–Acts, which portrays tongues as an external sign of the Spirit's coming, and also by the more immediate context, which indicates Luke's encouragement to pray for the Holy Spirit is a response to the fears of some within his community. This text, then, indicates that Luke viewed tongues as positive and available to every disciple of Jesus.

---

[22] It is perhaps significant that Luke's comparisons feature dangerous objects ('snake' and 'scorpion', Lk. 11.11-12), where as Matthew's comparisons include one that is simply useless ('stone' and 'snake', Mt. 7.9-10). This might suggest that Luke was consciously seeking to help his readers overcome their fear.

[23] For Jewish and pagan examples of ecstasy and inspired utterances see Dunn, *Jesus and the Spirit*, pp. 304-305.

[24] Note that the Beelzebub controversy immediately follows (Lk. 11.14-28). Some accused Jesus of being demon-possessed (Lk. 11.15). The early Christians were undoubtedly confronted with similar charges. It is thus not surprising that Luke 'takes pains to show [that] Christianity [is] both different from and superior to magic' (Richard Vinson, *Luke* [Macon, GA: Smyth & Helwys Publishing, 2008], p. 380; cf. Acts 8.9-24; 16.16-18; 19.11-20).

Conclusion

I have argued that, according to Luke, tongues played a significant role in the life of the apostolic church. Furthermore, Luke expected that tongues would continue to play a positive role in his church and ours, both of which are located in 'these last days'. In Luke's view, every believer can manifest this spiritual gift. So, Luke encourages every believer to pray for prophetic anointings (Lk. 11.13), experiences of Spirit-inspired exultation from which power and praise flow; experiences similar to those modeled by Jesus (Lk. 3.21-22; 10.21) and the early church (Acts 2.4; 10.46; 19.6). Luke believed that these experiences would typically include glossolalia, which he considered a special form of prophetic speech and a sign that the Pentecostal gift had been received.

These conclusions are based on a number of interrelated arguments that might be summarized as follows:

1) Glossolalia was well known and widely practiced in the early church.

2) Luke's narrative reveals that he views speaking in tongues as a special type of prophetic speech.

3) Luke indicates that glossolalia, as a special type of prophetic speech, has an ongoing role to play in the life of the church.

4) Luke presents Jesus' experience of the Spirit and his life of prayer, including a significant moment of spiritual rapture in which he bursts forth with joyful praise (Lk. 10.21), as important models for his readers.

5) Luke highlights in a unique way the importance and necessity of Spirit-inspired praise: praise and bold witness go hand in hand, they are both the necessary and inevitable consequence of being filled with the Holy Spirit.

6) Luke views the Pentecostal outpouring of the Spirit as a fulfillment of Moses' wish (Num. 11.29) and Joel's prophecy (Joel 2.28-32). Thus, it is a prophetic anointing that is marked by the ecstatic speech characteristic of prophets (i.e. glossolalia).

7) According to Luke, the gift of tongues is available to every disciple of Jesus; thus, Luke encourages believers to pray for a prophetic anointing, which he envisions will include glossolalia.

These conclusions suggest that Luke presents a challenge to the contemporary church – a church that has all too often lost sight of its apostolic calling and charismatic roots. Glossolalia, in a unique way, symbolizes this challenge. It reminds us of our calling and our need of divine enabling. This was true of Luke's church and it is equally true of ours. Put another way, tongues remind us of our true identity: we are to be a community of prophets, called and empowered to bear bold witness for Jesus and to declare his mighty deeds.

It should not surprise us, then, that the gift of tongues serves as an important symbol for modern Pentecostals. Just as this experience connected Luke's church with its apostolic roots; so also tongues serves a similar purpose for Pentecostals today. It symbolizes and validates our approach to the book of Acts: its stories become 'our' stories. This in turn encourages us to reconsider our apostolic calling and our charismatic heritage. In short, for Pentecostals tongues serve as a sign that the calling and power of the apostolic church is valid for believers today.

Application

Brother Yang is a graduate of an 'underground' Bible school in China. Since his graduation he has led many from various unreached people groups to Christ. On this particular day as I spoke with him, he described his experience as if it had happened yesterday. He told of how when he was praying as a young student at the Bible school over a decade ago, he heard a voice directing him to proclaim the gospel to those who had not yet heard. He declared, 'that voice has remained with me until this day'. Speaking in tongues had become a regular part of his prayer life and he also noted how when he spoke in tongues, he felt strengthened and encouraged to pursue this call that had come to him – the call to take the gospel to those who had never heard it.

Some months later I was privileged to baptize Brother Yang's friend, Brother Yu. As Brother Yu stood waist deep in the cool water of a beautiful lake in Southwest China, he shared about his background and how he came to a vital, life-changing faith in Christ at the Bible school. Brother Yu certainly exudes a vibrant faith, one that has been nurtured by his commitment to prayer. During one of these moments of fervent prayer, Brother Yu was filled with the Holy Spirit like the disciples on the day of Pentecost (Acts 2.4). While he prayed in tongues, he saw a vision that greatly encouraged him. In the vision he saw that he was presenting the gospel to people who had never heard about Jesus! Brother Yu does not know exactly where the Lord will lead him, but he emerged from those baptismal waters confident that God is directing his steps. I believe that he and Brother Yang are travelling down the same road. And it is no coincidence that their sense of call, this passion to take the good news of Jesus to those who have never heard, is connected with experiences where, deeply moved by the Holy Spirit, they have burst forth uttering languages that they did not understand. You see, speaking in tongues reminds us that, just like those first century believers, we too have been called to take the gospel 'to the ends of the earth' (Acts 1.8).

Reflection Questions

1. Luke's narrative emphasizes that praise and bold witness are the necessary and inevitable consequence of being filled with the Holy Spirit. How does Lk. 19.39-40 highlight this fact? Does my life reflect this reality?

2. How does Lk. 10.1-16 help us understand why tongues serve as a special sign in the narrative of Acts? Might this sign be edifying and encouraging to us as well?

3. Menzies argues that Luke's inspired and skillful presentation of Jesus' teaching on prayer in Lk. 11.9-13 is shaped by his desire to encourage every reader (every believer) to pray for a prophetic anointing – an anointing of the Spirit that Luke envisions will include speaking in tongues. Do you understand why this is the case? Have you asked the Lord for this kind of anointing?

4. According to the author, Luke presents a challenge to the contemporary church – a church that has all too often lost sight of its apostolic calling and charismatic roots. How does speaking in tongues symbolize this challenge?

PART TWO

JESUS AND TONGUES

INTRODUCTION

In the following two chapters, I would like to explore what the New Testament has to say about Jesus' experience of and attitude towards speaking in tongues. This topic may sound rather strange to some. Is there any biblical material here to discuss? Undoubtedly many without much thought would say 'no'. However, I do believe that this response is inadequate. In fact, I believe that two key passages shed important light on this topic. These passages are Lk. 10.21 and Mk 16.17. Let's begin our inquiry by looking at Lk. 10.21.

3

JESUS, TONGUES, AND THE MESSIANIC READING OF PSALM 16

Our study of Luke–Acts has revealed that the biblical pedigree of speaking in tongues is rather impressive. This phenomenon was not strange or exotic in the eyes of the apostolic church; on the contrary, speaking in tongues was widely practiced and held in high esteem by, at the very least, broad sectors of the New Testament church.[1] Furthermore, if Luke and Paul are to be our guides (rather than Calvin and Warfield), it would appear that they felt that speaking in tongues had an ongoing role to play in the life of the church.

This acknowledgment raises an interesting and important question. How did this positive perspective on speaking in tongues develop? Or, perhaps put more clearly, how did the early Christians affirm and give Scriptural support for their practice of speaking in tongues? Certainly we would expect that after joyful moments of spiritual exultation marked by glossolalia, the early church would have sought to ground their experience in the Old Testament. This is precisely what we find happening in their understanding of Jesus and the mission that Jesus called them to embrace (Acts 13.33-37, 47). But what Old Testament texts did the early church draw upon to support their practice of speaking in tongues? And what role, if any, did Jesus play in this process? This is the focus of the following chapter.

---

[1] For a similar judgment, see Dunn, *Jesus and the Spirit*, pp. 245-46.

Jesus Our Model

We have already noted that Luke views speaking in tongues as a special type of prophetic speech that has an ongoing role in the life of the church. Additionally, Luke sees this type of exuberant, inspired speech modeled in the life of Jesus. This is clearly the case in Lk. 10.21: 'At that time Jesus, full of joy through the Holy Spirit, said, "I praise you, Father, Lord of heaven and earth …"'[2]

In Chapter One we noted the striking manner in which Luke introduces Jesus' words of praise: 'he rejoiced in the Holy Spirit and said' (ἠγαλλιάσατο ἐν τῷ πνεύματι τῷ ἁγίῳ καὶ εἶπεν; Lk. 10.21).[3] Here Luke utilizes the verb ἀγαλλιάω (rejoice), which appears frequently in the LXX. The verb is especially prominent in the Psalms and the poetic portions of the Prophets and denotes spiritual exultation that issues forth in praise to God for his mighty acts.[4] It is important to note that the subject of the verb is not simply ushered into a state of sacred rapture; he also 'declares the acts of God'.[5] The connection between ἀγαλλιάω and the declaration of the mighty acts of God is particularly striking in Luke–Acts.[6] The verb describes the joyful praise of Mary (Lk. 1.47), Jesus (Lk. 10.21), and David (Acts 2.26) in response to God's salvific activity in Jesus. In Lk. 1.47 and 10.21 the verb is specifically linked to the inspiration of the Holy Spirit, and in Acts 2.25-30 David is described as a prophet. This verb, then, was for Luke a particularly appropriate way of describing prophetic activity.

The reference in Acts 2.26 is especially important for our purposes; for here, the verb ἀγαλλιάω is associated with the word γλῶσσα (tongue). In a quotation from Ps. 16.9 (Ps. 15.9, LXX), Peter cites David as saying, 'Therefore my heart is glad and my tongue

---

[2] The key phrase, 'he rejoiced in the Holy Spirit' (Lk. 10.21; ASV), is unique to Luke. The saying that follows is paralleled in Mt. 11.25-27. The words of Jesus recorded in Lk. 10.21-22 also show unique points of contact with the Johannine tradition and thus this saying has been called the 'bolt from the Johannine blue'.

[3] I am following the *American Standard Version* here for the English translation.

[4] Bultmann, 'ἀγαλλιάομαι', p. 19; Morrice, *Joy in the New Testament*, p. 20.

[5] Bultmann, 'ἀγαλλιάομαι', p. 20.

[6] The linkage is made explicit in three out of four occurrences of the verb (Lk. 1.47; 10.21; Acts 2.26). The only exception is Acts 16.34.

rejoices (καὶ ἠγαλλιάσατο ἡ γλῶσσά μου) ...'[7] The coupling of ἀγαλλιάω with γλῶσσα is not unexpected, for six of the eight references to γλῶσσα in Luke–Acts describe experiences of spiritual exultation that result in praise.[8] It is evident that for Luke, ἀγαλλιάω and γλῶσσα, especially when associated with the inspiration of the Holy Spirit, are terms that describe special instances of prophetic inspiration, instances of spiritual exultation that produce jubilant praise.

We can say with confidence that Lk. 10.21 describes Jesus' prayer of thanksgiving in terms reminiscent of speaking in tongues: inspired by the Spirit, Jesus bursts forth in exuberant and joyful praise. Additionally, we may conclude that this description of Jesus' prayer life is not without purpose. It ties into a larger motif that runs throughout Luke's narrative. Luke presents Jesus' Spirit-inspired prophetic ministry, including his bold proclamation and exultant praise, as a model for his readers.[9]

It is quite possible, however, that Luke intends to say more. In view of the fact that the verb ἀγαλλιάω implies speech and elsewhere stands alone as a reference to praise,[10] Lk. 10.21, which references two verbs of speech, 'he *rejoiced* in the Holy Spirit and *said*' (ἠγαλλιάσατο ἐν τῷ πνεύματι τῷ ἁγίῳ καὶ εἶπεν), may suggest the occurrence of two distinct types of speech.[11] The verb ἀγαλλιάω, linked as it is to the inspiration of the Holy Spirit, may imply glossolalia; while the phrase, 'and he said' (καὶ εἶπεν), introduces the intelligible words of praise described in the narrative. This conclusion is supported by the manner in which speaking in tongues is described in Acts 10.46 ('speaking in tongues and praising God') and 19.6 ('they spoke in tongues and prophesied'), where

---

[7] It should be noted that here the LXX refers to 'tongue', whereas the MT reads 'glory'.

[8] These six are: Lk. 1.64; Acts 2.4, 11, 26; 10.46; 19.6. The other two references to γλῶσσα are found in Lk. 16.24 and Acts 2.3.

[9] Luke's emphasis on prayer, and particularly the prayers and prayer-life of Jesus, is widely recognized by contemporary scholars. Luke also associates prayer with the Holy Spirit in a unique way (e.g. Lk. 3.21-22; 11.13; Acts 4.31).

[10] Praise is clearly indicated by the verb in Lk. 1.47 and Acts 2.26; and it may be implied in Acts 16.34 as well.

[11] Notice Lk. 13.12, where the verb προσφωνέω ('to call') combined with καὶ εἶπεν clearly describes a separate action. Thus, the NIV translates: '... he called her forward and said to her, "Woman, ..."'

both texts may describe the pairing of glossolalia with other forms of intelligible speech. Admittedly, all of this is somewhat speculative and our suggestions at this point can only be put forward in a tentative manner. More important, however, is the link to Acts 2.26, which calls for further explanation.

Tongues and the Messianic Reading of Psalm 16

In Acts 2 Peter begins his sermon by announcing that the cacophony which has astonished the crowd is not, as some had charged, the ramblings of drunken men. It is rather the fulfillment of Joel's prophecy that in the last days God would pour out the Spirit of prophecy on his servants, both male and female. Peter then argues that, since these 'servants of the Lord' are the disciples of Jesus, this constitutes proof that God has raised Jesus from the dead and that he is Messiah and Lord.

Peter's argument at one critical point includes a reference to Ps. 16.8-11, which is cited in Acts 2.25-28. Peter declares that although his audience, 'with the help of wicked men', put Jesus to death by nailing him to a cross, 'God raised him from the dead … because it was impossible for death to keep its hold on him' (Acts 2.24). Peter then introduces the quote from Psalm 16.

> David said about him,
> "'I saw the Lord always before me.
> Because he is at my right hand,
> I will not be shaken.
> Therefore my heart is glad and my tongue rejoices (καὶ ἠγαλ-
> λιάσατο ἡ γλῶσσά μου);
> my body also will live in hope,
> because you will not abandon me to the grave,
> nor will you let your Holy One see decay.
> You have made known to me the paths of life;
> You will fill me with joy in your presence.'" (Acts 2.25-28)

After quoting these words, Peter declares that this Psalm must be interpreted as a prophecy uttered by David concerning the Messiah. Peter's logic is clear. David 'died and was buried', but 'he was a prophet' and knew that God had promised to place 'one of his descendants on his throne' (Acts 2.29-30). Indeed, 'Seeing what was ahead, he spoke of … the Christ' (Acts 2.31).

Peter's interpretation indicates that the early Christians read these verses as if the Messiah was the subject (that is, the speaker), not David. In other words, the early church read Ps. 16.8-11 as a description of Jesus. It is Jesus' tongue that rejoices and it is his body that was not abandoned to the grave. The verses from Psalm 16 cited here include the phrase, 'my tongue rejoices' (καὶ ἠγαλ-λιάσατο ἡ γλῶσσά μου) as well as key references to the resurrection, such as 'you will not abandon me to the grave' (Acts 2.26-27; cf. 2.31). Although Peter's interpretation clearly highlights the references to the resurrection,[12] it should not be missed, particularly in light of the larger context of Luke–Acts, that Ps. 16.9 (Ps. 15.9, LXX) also refers to the rejoicing of Jesus' tongue and in language that echoes Lk. 10.21. Indeed, the reference to 'my tongue rejoices' in Ps. 16.9 suggests that Luke's description of Jesus' exultation and inspired speech in Lk. 10.21, a text unique to Luke's gospel, serves a significant literary and theological purpose. It anticipates the reference to 'my tongue rejoices' (καὶ ἠγαλλιάσατο ἡ γλῶσσά μου) in the Psalm cited by Peter (Acts 2.26), which the early church read prophetically of Jesus, and demonstrates that the prophecy it contains was fulfilled in the ministry of Jesus.[13] This much, I hope to establish, can be argued with considerable force.

However, it is quite possible that we should glean more from these texts. Given the literary connections which tie the reference to 'my tongue rejoices' in Acts 2.26 together, on the one hand, with Jesus' Spirit-inspired exultation in Lk. 10.21 and, on the other hand, with the 'speaking in tongues' of Acts 2.4, 10.46, and 19.6, the reference to 'my tongue rejoices' might also suggest that Luke and the early church read this phrase from Ps. 16.9 as a reference to speaking in tongues, which they understood to have been practiced by Jesus.

It spite of the literary connections noted above, the bulk of contemporary scholarship has remained largely blind to this reading of

---

[12] Paul also presents Psalm 16.10 (Psalm 15.10, LXX) as a prophecy of Jesus' resurrection in his sermon at Pisidian Antioch in Acts 13.35-37.

[13] This connection between Jesus' experience (Luke 10.21) and a messianic reading of 'my tongue rejoices' (Psalm 15.9, LXX) must have been made in a Hellenistic setting, since only the LXX refers here to 'tongue' (the MT reads 'glory').

the text. The key reason for this is the tendency to read Peter's quotation of Ps. 16.8-11 as referring to prophetic words of the Messiah that are fulfilled only at the moment of Jesus' resurrection and exaltation.[14] More specifically, the key phrases, 'my tongue rejoices' (Acts 2.26/Ps. 16.9) and 'you will fill me with joy in your presence' (πληρώσεις με εὐφροσύνης μετὰ τοῦ προσώπου σου, Acts 2.28/Ps. 16.11) are either ignored as irrelevant[15] or interpreted as pointing to Jesus' exaltation and read as if the Messiah utters them from his exalted position at the right hand of the Father (Acts 2.33).[16] The scholarly consensus, however, generally fails to acknowledge or address two crucial and interrelated questions: (1) Why does Luke cite the extended, non-resurrection parts of the quotation from Ps. 16.8-11?, and (2) When are the phrases 'my tongue rejoices' and 'you will fill me with joy in your presence' fulfilled, during Jesus' earthly ministry or only at his exaltation in heaven?

I contend that a careful reading of this passage indicates that we should read these phrases, 'my tongue rejoices' and 'you will fill me

---

[14] Most commentators focus on the resurrection phrases in Acts 2.27/Ps. 16.10, which are referenced again by Peter in Acts 2.31, and ignore the other elements of the Psalm cited in Acts 2.25-28. Thus David Moessner writes, 'The conventional exegesis of this lengthy citation … regards Psalm 15.8-11 as an explanation *only* of the resurrection' ('Two Lords "at the Right Hand"? The Psalms and an Intertextual Reading of Peter's Pentecost Speech [Acts 2.14-36]', in Richard Thompson and Thomas Phillips (eds.), *Literary Studies in Luke–Acts: Essays in Honor of Joseph B. Tyson* [Macon, GA: Mercy University Press, 1998], p. 221, italics his).

[15] Speaking of the phrases 'my heart is glad' and 'my tongue rejoices' (Ps. 15.9, LXX/Acts 2.26), C.K. Barrett concludes: 'These two clauses, thought apt in the Psalm, do not bear upon the argument in Acts; they are included because they are in the text quoted' (*The Acts of the Apostles, Vol. 1* [London: T&T Clark International, 1994 (2004 edn)], p. 145). So also Ben Witherington III states, 'The emphasis here is not on demonstrating that Jesus fulfilled Scripture;' rather, Luke highlights that Jesus' death and resurrection were a part of God's plan (*The Acts of the Apostles: A Socio-Rhetorical Commentary* [Grand Rapids: Eerdmans, 1998], p. 146). Darrell L. Bock, referring to the change in Ps. 15.9, LXX to 'tongue' from the MT's 'glory', states, 'This change is of no significance to the argument' (*Proclamation from Prophecy and Pattern: Lucan Old Testament Christology* [JSNTSS 12; Sheffield: JSOT Press, 1987], pp. 172-73).

[16] See, for example, Joseph A. Fitzmyer, *The Acts of the Apostles* (The Anchor Yale Bible; New Haven, CT: Yale University Press, 1998), pp. 256-57; Ernst Haenchen, *The Acts of the Apostles* (Philadelphia: The Westminster Press, 1971), pp. 181-82; and Craig S. Keener, *Acts: An Exegetical Commentary, Vol. 1* (Grand Rapids: Baker Academic, 2012), pp. 944-50.

with joy in your presence', as pointing to experiences that take place during Jesus' ministry. Indeed, the entire quotation from Ps. 16.8-11 is best understood when it is read as a pronouncement uttered by Jesus during his earthly ministry that extolls his intimate and joyful relationship with the Father and expresses his unwavering hope in the resurrection. The key reasons for seeing the references, 'my tongue rejoices' and 'you will fill me with joy in your presence', as referring to events that take place during Jesus' ministry include the following:

1. The reference to 'he is at my right hand' (Acts 2.25) should not be seen as a reference to Jesus' exalted state because there Jesus is seated at the Father's right hand. As Keener notes, 'one can hardly be at another's right hand and have that person at one's own right hand' (cf. Acts 2.33-34).[17] A different Old Testament passage, Psalm 110, is invoked as Scriptural proof of Christ's exaltation. Rather, this text (Acts 2.25) refers to Jesus' intimate relationship with the Father during his earthly ministry.[18] This results in his heart being glad and his 'tongue' rejoicing (2.26).

2. This judgment is supported by the impressive literary connections between Lk. 10.21 and Acts 2.26. The verb ἀγαλλιάω is rarely used by Luke, and its use in Lk. 10.21 is clearly the result of Lukan redaction: the parallels between Luke and Matthew reflect an underlying tradition into which Luke has inserted the phrase, 'he rejoiced in the Holy Spirit'. This makes the link between Lk. 10.21 and Acts 2.26 all the more significant. Additionally, the verb is explicitly linked to the Holy Spirit in Lk. 10.21, as are the inspired 'tongues' of Acts 2.4, 11. In this context the ref-

---

[17] Keener, *Acts*, p. 947 (although Keener goes on to interpret the references to 'right hand' [Acts 2.25 and 2.34] as metaphorical, and thus still connects vv. 25-26 with Jesus' exaltation). Note also I. Howard Marshall, who concludes, 'sitting at the right hand of Yahweh … is not in mind at this point' ('Acts', in G.K. Beale and D.A. Carson (eds.), *Commentary on the New Testament Use of the Old Testament* [Grand Rapids: Baker Academic, 2007], p. 537).

[18] Contra Moessner ('Two Lords', pp. 222-32), in Acts 2.25 (Ps. 16.8) 'the Lord' refers to God the Father, while the subject ('I saw … before me') is identified as Jesus (cf. Acts 2.29-31). In Acts 2.34 (Ps. 110.1), 'The Lord' also refers to God the Father, while 'my Lord' refers to Jesus.

erence to 'my tongue rejoices' (Acts 2.26) clearly evokes speech inspired by the Holy Spirit (i.e. glossolalia).

3. This judgment finds further support in Jesus' ecstatic[19] experience described in Luke 10.21, which produces a dramatic, revelatory declaration that highlights his unique relationship to the Father and his lofty status as the Son (Luke 10.21-22).[20] Thus, in addition to the literary parallels cited above, there is a unique and impressive conceptual link between Luke 10.21-22 and Psalm 16.8-11: both texts highlight the close, intimate relationship between the Father and the Son.

4. Additionally, this conclusion is affirmed by the strong associations between the Holy Spirit, the verb 'to fill' (πληρόω),[21] and 'joy' (εὐφροσύνη)[22] that are characteristic of Luke–Acts. These associations, particularly in the context of Acts 2 with its multiple references and allusions to Spirit-inspired 'tongues', also encourage the reader to interpret the phrase 'you will fill me with joy in your presence' as referring to Jesus' ecstatic experience of the Spirit during his earthly ministry. Again, Lk. 10.21 is probably the central text in view, although the reader might also think of other texts (Lk. 3.21-22; 4.1, 14) as well.

5. The verb tenses, especially the future tense of the verbs in the key phrases that speak of the resurrection of the body, 'my body also *will live* in hope', 'you *will not abandon* me to the grave', and 'nor *will you let* your Holy One see decay',[23] suggest that the Mes-

---

[19] With the term, 'ecstatic', I mean 'pertaining to or flowing from an experience of intense joy'. I do not wish to imply a loss of control with this term. While glossolalia transcends our reasoning faculties, the experience does not render them useless (cf. 1 Cor. 14.28, 32-33).

[20] The so-called 'bolt from the Johannine blue'.

[21] The Holy Spirit is associated with πληρόω/πίμπλημι in Lk. 1.15, 41, 67; Acts 2.4; 4.8, 31; 9.17; 13.9, 52.

[22] Luke's vocabulary for terms associated with joy and rejoicing is rich and varied. References to joy permeate his narrative and are frequently associated with prophecy, prophetic or revelatory pronouncements, and the Holy Spirit (Lk. 1.14, 28, 44, 47; 2.10; 6.23; 10.17, 21; 19.37; Acts 2.26, 28; 5.41; 13.52).

[23] The verbs, κατασκηνόω (to live), ἐγκαταλείπω (to abandon), δίδωμι (to give or allow) are all in the future tense (LXX, Ps. 15.9-10). The italics are mine. Note the shift to the aorist tense in Peter's explanation of these verses (Acts 2.31).

siah speaks these words prior to his resurrection and exaltation.[24] A messianic reading of Psalm 16 is thus most coherent if it is read as a saying of Jesus uttered during his earthly ministry.[25]

6. This reading of Psalm 16 is consistent with Luke's use of Old Testament prophecy elsewhere. In the quotation of Joel 2.28-32, recorded in Acts 2.17-21, we encounter an Old Testament prophecy that finds fulfillment in the ministry of Jesus, but that also anticipates an ongoing fulfillment in the ministry of Jesus' disciples. Note for example how the 'signs and wonders' of Joel's prophecy (Acts 2.19) anticipate the miracles of Jesus (Acts 2.22) as well as miracles performed by various followers of Jesus (Acts 2.43; 4.30; 5.12; 6.8; 14.3; 15.12). The same may be said for Joel's references to end-time prophets (Acts 2.17-18), which find fulfillment both in Luke's Gospel (e.g. Lk. 4.18-19) and throughout the book of Acts (e.g. Acts 4.8, 31). This approach to Old Testament prophecy anticipates the early church's messianic reading of Psalm 16, which highlights the fulfillment of 'my tongue rejoices' in the ministry of Jesus, but which also points to an ongoing fulfillment in the experience of Jesus' disciples.

7. The fact that in Luke's account Peter begins the quotation from Psalm 16 at v. 8 and ends at v. 11 is also striking and significant. Luke easily could have focused more narrowly on the key references to the resurrection of the body found in vv. 9b-11a as he does with Paul in Acts 13.35-37.[26] The reason for citing the extended quotation appears to be the focus in vv. 8-9a and v. 11b on joyful, ecstatic experience, which anticipates the disciples' experience of inspired tongues-speech cited in Acts 2.33, 'what

---

[24] The NRSV translates the aorist verbs of Acts 2.26 (εὐφραίνω and ἀγαλλιάω) by using the past tense: 'my heart was glad, and my tongue rejoiced'. However, even if this reading is adopted, it would only suggest that the early Christians read the Psalm as if it were uttered by Jesus after the experience of Lk. 10.21, but prior to his death and resurrection.

[25] While it is possible that the future tense of the verb in the phrase, 'you will fill me with joy in your presence' (Acts 2.28), points forward to Jesus' exaltation, in view of the other factors outlined above I would argue that the use of the future tense here was most likely understood as referring to events or experiences that took place during Jesus' ministry.

[26] Paul presents essentially the same argument for Jesus' resurrection as does Peter, but he only cites the phrase from Ps. 16.10, 'You will not let your Holy One see decay' (Acts 13.35).

you now see and hear'. This judgment is strengthened by the fact that Luke omits the final line of Ps. 16.11 from his quotation, 'with eternal pleasures at your right hand' (τερπνότητες ἐν τῇ δεξιᾷ σου εἰς τέλος).[27] Again, this suggests that Luke's focus at this point is on Jesus' intimate, joyful experience rather than his exalted position in heaven at the Father's right hand.

8. Finally, it should be noted that while Luke's argument for Jesus' resurrection is rooted in Psalm 16 with its related references to Jesus' experience and his resurrection (Acts 2.25-32), his argument for Jesus' exaltation (Acts 2.33-36) is rooted in Psalm 110 and the experience of the disciples (i.e. their Spirit-inspired 'tongues'). It is the focus on 'experience', Jesus' experience and that of his disciples, that unites Psalm 16 and the argument for Jesus' resurrection with the disciples' experience and the argument for Jesus' exaltation.[28] This emphasis on joyful, charismatic experience suggests that Luke was also consciously appealing to the experience of his readers. It indicates that Luke has carefully crafted his summary of Peter's sermon with an eye to presenting Jesus' ecstatic exultation, an experience that Luke probably understood as including 'speaking in tongues' (i.e., glossolalia), as

---

[27] Numerous scholars suggest that Luke follows the rabbinic *gezerah shavah* hermeneutic, which links together two citations by their use of a common term. The reference to 'my right hand' in Ps. 16.8 (Acts 2.25), which links with 'my right hand' in Ps. 110.1 (Acts 2.34), is thus presented as the reason that Luke begins the quotation at this point. However, Luke could have easily omitted Ps. 16.8-9 and maintained the verbal link by simply quoting the full text of Ps. 16.10-11, since v. 11 also refers to 'your right hand'. Clearly, the content of Ps. 16.8-9 was important for Luke's purposes.

[28] This section (Acts 2.25-36) appears to exhibit an A, B, C, B', A' structure:

A. *Joyful Experience*: 'my heart is glad'/'my tongue rejoices' (2.25-26).

B. *Resurrection*: 'you will not abandon me to the grave'/'nor will you let your Holy One see decay' (2.27).

C. *Resurrection and Joyful Experience*: 'you have made known to me the paths of life' (resurrection; 2.28a); 'you will fill me with joy in your presence' (joyful, ecstatic experience, implying tongues; 2.28b).

B.' *Resurrection*: an explanation of the key phrases from Ps. 16.10 ('you will not abandon me to the grave'/'nor will you let your Holy One see decay') which indicates that they should be read as references to Jesus' resurrection (2.29-32).

A.' *Joyful Experience*: an explanation of the tongues of 2.4 (cf. 2.11), 'what you now see and hear' (2.33), that presents them, in conjunction with the prophetic reading of Psalm 110, as proof that Jesus is the exalted Lord, who sits at the right hand of the Father (Acts 2.33-36).

both a fulfillment of prophecy (Psalm 16.9, 11) and as anticipating the experience of the disciples on the day of Pentecost, as
well as, no doubt, also anticipating the experience of many of his
readers.[29] Jesus' tongues, then, demonstrate, along with the
tongues of the disciples at Pentecost and the tongues of Luke's
community, that he is the exalted Lord.

In short, it would appear that the early church viewed Jesus' experience of glossolalia (implied in Lk. 10.21) as a fulfillment of Ps.
16.9, which they read as a messianic prophecy. This means that the
miraculous tongues of Jesus' disciples not only serve as a proof of
Jesus' resurrection/exaltation and thus that he is Messiah and Lord
(cf. Acts 2.33: 'what you now see and hear'), but so also does Jesus'
own experience of glossolalia serve as a proof. It is a fulfillment of
one aspect of the messianic prophecy contained in Ps. 16.8-11. Furthermore, Jesus' experience of inspired speech (i.e. glossolalia) and
that of his disciples recorded in the book of Acts anticipates the
reader's experience and highlights that the 'tongues' inspired by the
Holy Spirit in their lives also serve as proof of Jesus' exalted status.
Although our assertion that the early church associated Jesus' Spirit-
inspired praise (Lk. 10.21) and the Messiah's 'joyful tongue' (Ps.
16.9) with speaking in tongues is less secure than our judgment that
Lk. 10.21 anticipates and fulfills a prophetic reading of Acts 2.26, it
does correlate with and help explain several distinctive features of
Luke–Acts and Luke's community.

The Logic of Acts 2.26 and Tongues in Acts

Tongues as a Sign. One of the striking features of Luke's narrative in
Acts is the conspicuous role played by speaking in tongues. Speaking in tongues is associated with prophecy and presented as a significant sign in each of the three passages which describe this phenomenon in Acts. The stage is set, the model unveiled, in Acts 2.

In Acts 2.17-18 (cf. Acts 2.4) speaking in tongues is specifically
described as a fulfillment of Joel's prophecy that in the last days all
of God's people will prophesy. The cacophony produced by the
tongues-speech of Jesus' disciples is not the result of too much rev-

---

[29] We shall develop the point that this passage anticipates the experience of
Luke's readers in the following section.

elry; rather, Peter explains, it is the sound of inspired utterances issued by God's end-time prophets (Acts 2.13, 15-17). The meaning
of the symbolism of the speaking 'in other tongues', which enables
'the Jews from every nation under heaven' to hear the message in
their 'own language' (Acts 2.5-6), is clearly explained. It marks this
group as members of Joel's end-time prophetic band and indicates
that the 'last days' and the salvation associated with it have arrived.
Thus, Luke narrates Peter's powerful declaration concerning Jesus,
'Exalted to the right hand of God … he [Jesus] has poured out *what
you now see and hear*' (Acts 2.33). 'Therefore', Peter declares, 'let all
Israel be assured of this: God has made this Jesus, whom you cruci-
fied, both Lord and Christ' (Acts 2.36). The logic of the narrative is
transparent. Since the Spirit of prophecy is only given to the 'servants' of God (Acts 2.18) – that is, the true people of God, the heirs
of the promise God made to Israel (Joel 2.28-32) – and, since the
disciples of Jesus are those who are now receiving this gift, it follows that Jesus is Lord (Acts 2.33) and that his disciples constitute
the true people of God. In Acts 2 tongues speech, then, serves as a
sign that both validates the disciples' claim that Jesus is Lord and
confirms their status as members of Joel's end-time prophetic
band.[30]

The association with prophecy is made again in Acts 10.42-48.
While Peter was still preaching to Cornelius and his household, the
Holy Spirit 'came on all those who heard the message' (Acts 10.44).
Peter's colleagues 'were astonished that the gift of the Holy Spirit
had been poured out even on the Gentiles, for they heard them
speaking in tongues and praising God' (Acts 10.45-46). Notice how
the Holy Spirit interrupts Peter just as he declares, 'He [Jesus]
commanded us to preach to the people and to testify that he is the
one whom God appointed as judge of the living and the dead. *All
the prophets testify about him* that everyone who believes in him receives forgiveness of sins through his name' (Acts 10.42-43). As we

---

[30] So E. Schweizer concludes that the phrase 'and you will receive the gift of
the Holy Spirit' (Acts 2.38) should be interpreted as a promise that the Spirit shall
be 'imparted to those who are already converted and baptized' (Schweizer,
'πνεῦμα', *TDNT*, VI, p. 412). Note also the judgment offered by S. Brown:
'Surely it is preferable to interpret the passage in accordance with all the other
texts which we have considered and to understand the words "you shall receive"
to point to an event subsequent to baptism' ('"Water-Baptism" and "Spirit-
Baptism" in Luke–Acts', *ATR* 59 [1977], p. 144).

have noted, it can hardly be coincidental that the Holy Spirit breaks in and inspires glossolalia precisely at this point in Peter's sermon. Indeed, when Cornelius and his household burst forth in tongues, this act provides demonstrative proof that they too are in fact part of the end-time prophetic band of which Joel prophesied. They too are prophets that 'testify' about Jesus. How, then, can Peter and the others withhold baptism from them?

Finally, in Acts 19.6 the connection between prophecy and speaking in tongues is again explicitly stated. When Paul laid hands on the Ephesian disciples, the Holy Spirit 'came on them, and they spoke in tongues and prophesied'. Here, again, tongues serves as a significant sign. Paul's prior question posed to the Ephesian 'disciples', 'Did you receive the Holy Spirit when you believed?' (Acts 19.2), implies another question, 'How would we know?' Of course the pattern and literary connections that Luke has created enable us to answer this question and anticipate the outcome that follows.

All of this demonstrates that Luke has carefully crafted his narrative in order to highlight the connections between Acts 2.4, 10.46, and 19.6. Luke creates this literary linkage by presenting, in each instance, 'speaking in tongues' as the definitive and expected sign for reception of the Spirit of prophecy promised by Joel. This sign confirms that the disciples are the true people of God and also validates their proclamation that Jesus is Lord.

The logic of Luke's narrative, which centers on 'speaking in tongues' as a sign, fits beautifully with a messianic reading of Ps. 16.9 that understands Jesus' own experience of glossolalia, implied in Lk. 10.21, as a fulfillment of the prophecy that the Messiah's tongue would rejoice. On this reading, just as tongues serve as a sign for those who are a part of the end-time community of prophets, so also tongues mark the ultimate prophet and source of this prophetic community.

Luke, more than any other evangelist, highlights the fact that Jesus is a prophet.[31] Jesus, the prophet like Moses (Acts 3.22; 7.37), is the supreme example of what it means to be a prophet. Luke not only emphasizes Jesus' prophetic anointing and power (Lk. 4.14-21; cf. Acts 2.22, 10.38), he also stresses the necessity of Jesus' suffer-

---

[31] Luke 4.24; 7.16, 39; 13.33; 22.64; 24.19; Acts 3.22; 7.37.

ing, which was foretold by the prophets.[32] As the narrative unfolds, it becomes clear that Jesus' disciples will share his prophetic anointing, and they too will also share his suffering.[33] With these features of Luke's narrative in view, our suggested reading of 'my tongue rejoices' (Acts 2.26) as referencing Jesus' own experience of glossolalia appears highly appropriate. This is particularly the case when we remember that: (1) the verb ἀγαλλιάω is rarely used by Luke,[34] which makes the link between Lk. 10.21 and Acts 2.26 all the more significant; (2) the verb is explicitly linked to the Holy Spirit in Lk. 10.21; and (3) tongues-speech plays a special role in the narrative in Acts.

The Expectation of Tongues in Luke's Community. We have noted that for Luke tongues serve as a sign. This sign confirms that the disciples are the true people of God and validates their proclamation. I would add that this sort of apologetic suggests that Luke's readers routinely experienced this sign themselves. If 'speaking in tongues' was relatively unknown to Luke's readers, this message – that tongues validated their proclamation and standing before God – would carry little encouragement. However, if they too experienced glossolalia, then the dialogue in Luke's narrative takes on fresh meaning.[35] Peter's declaration that they 'have received the Holy Spirit just as we have' (Acts 10.47) speaks directly to Luke's readers and reminds them of the apostolic calling and power that is also theirs. Paul's question, 'Did you receive the Holy Spirit when you believed?' (Acts 19.2), encourages Luke's readers to reflect on their experiences of Spirit-inspired rapture and recognize that their own

---

[32] Texts that specifically refer to Jesus' suffering as foretold by the prophets include Lk. 16.31; 18.31-32; 24.25-27, 44-46; Acts 3.18; 7.52; 13.27; 26.22-23; cf. Acts 10.39-43; 28.23.

[33] Paul Minear describes 'Luke's two volumes as an account of the training of apprentice seers and exorcists' and then speaks of 'a succession of prophets from Abel to Paul … linked together by divine purpose and human suffering' (Paul S. Minear, *To Heal and To Reveal: The Prophetic Vocation According to Luke* [New York: The Seabury Press, 1976], pp. 148-49).

[34] The verb appears eleven times in the NT; four in Luke–Acts.

[35] Robert Tannehill notes that in his sermon recorded in Acts 2 'Peter appeals to his hearers' own experience, to what they themselves know, see, and hear (2.22, 29, 33), which can be an especially convincing basis for an argument' (*Luke–Acts*, p. 41). Tannehill does not seem to consider that this appeal to experience might also be directed to Luke's readers.

expressions of tongues-speech mark them as end-time prophets, people called and empowered to bear witness for Jesus.

The suggestion that Luke's readers routinely experienced tongues finds further support in Luke's redaction of Jesus' teaching on prayer, recorded in Lk. 11.13: 'If you then, though you are evil, know how to give good gifts to your children, how much more will your Father in heaven give the Holy Spirit to those who ask Him!' We have already noted how Luke, through his skillful editing of this saying, encourages post-Pentecostal disciples to pray for a prophetic anointing, an experience similar to those modeled by Jesus (Lk. 3.21-22; 10.21) and the early church (Acts 2.4; 10.46; 19.6). Luke's readers would naturally expect glossolalia to be a normal, frequent, and expected part of this experience. This judgment is confirmed by the immediate context, which reveals that Luke's encouragement to pray for the Holy Spirit is designed to quell the fears of some within his community, as well as the larger context of Luke–Acts.

This insight into Luke's perspective and that of his readers brings us back to the questions we raised at the beginning of our essay. How did this positive perspective on speaking in tongues develop? What role did Jesus play in this process? And, more specifically, what Old Testament texts did the early church draw upon to support their practice of speaking in tongues?

Undoubtedly a key text that encouraged the early Christians in their experience of tongues was Joel 2.28-32, cited in Acts 2.17-21. We have also suggested that Num. 11.24-30, which forms the backdrop for Lk. 10.1, informed their practice of glossolalia. Yet these texts lack any explicit reference to tongues. Psalm 16.9, however, provides the early church with precisely what it needed. The literary connections between Jesus' inspired praise (Lk. 10.21) and Ps. 16.9, along with the verbal links between this verse, with its reference to 'my tongue rejoices', and the key texts in Acts that reference speaking in tongues (Acts 2.4, 10.46, 19.6), suggest that a messianic reading of Ps. 16.9 provided the early church with its Scriptural rationale for speaking in tongues. This text presents Jesus as the model for their experience of tongues and also grounds this experience in Old Testament prophecy. All of this suggests that a messianic reading of Ps. 16.9 played an important role in the formation of the early church's positive appraisal and enthusiastic embrace of their experience of speaking in tongues.

The Ambiguity of the Evidence. The question must be asked, if indeed the early church read Ps. 16.9 as a prophecy of the Messiah and they saw this prophecy as being fulfilled in Jesus' own experience, why then did they not highlight more clearly the fact that Jesus spoke in tongues? I believe that there are two answers to this question, two ways to explain the lack of information on this point. First, it would appear that there were not any traditions or stories that explicitly described Jesus speaking in tongues. This should not surprise us, for much of the material recorded in the gospels has to do either with Jesus' teaching or events from his public ministry. Jesus' experience of speaking in tongues would not readily fit into either one of these categories. Tongues-speech does not lend itself to description. There would not be any specific content to record and pass on. Additionally, Jesus' glossolalic praise would generally have been exercised in private or in the company of a select few. As it is, we have little information about Jesus' prayer life. This being the case, it is not surprising that Luke should provide us with the deepest insights here, since he more than any other gospel writer highlights Jesus' practice of praying and his prayers. So, we should not make too much out of the fact that none of the gospel writers state the matter explicitly or that, as we have suggested, Luke merely implies Jesus' experience of tongues. It may well be that Luke was aware of the general fact that Jesus did speak in tongues, but that he did not have any specific traditions or stories that highlighted this fact.[36]

Secondly, it is also possible that the early church did not view this matter with totally unanimity. As I have noted, the fact that Luke needs to encourage his readers to pray for the prophetic gift suggests that there may have been some who had reservations about this experience (Lk. 11.13). Although speaking in tongues appears to have been widely practiced in the early church, it is entirely possible that some groups were less open to this manifestation of the Spirit's inspiration than others. This, too, might account for

---

[36] The disciples might not have understood or attached significance to Jesus' experiences of glossolalia until after their own similar experiences at Pentecost and beyond. This, too, might account for the paucity of traditional material describing Jesus' experience of glossolalia. In any event, Luke's unwillingness to read back into the life of Jesus explicit references to glossolalia is an argument for the historical reliability of Luke–Acts.

the lack of specific traditions that reference Jesus' experience of tongues. An experience that is not understood or valued is an experience that is not likely to be recounted and passed on.

In any event, it seems that students of the Bible need to look at this issue with fresh lenses. We need to account for the fact that speaking in tongues was well known, widely practiced, and generally held in high esteem in the early church. My own tentative proposal is offered with the hope that it will encourage further reflection on this practice that marked the life of the early church and continues to encourage Christians today.

Conclusion

By way of summary, I offer the following conclusions. First, the reference to 'my tongue rejoices' in Ps. 16.9 suggests that Luke's description of Jesus' exultation and inspired speech in Lk. 10.21, a text unique to Luke's gospel, serves a significant literary and theological purpose. It anticipates the reference to 'my tongue rejoices' (καὶ ἠγαλλιάσατο ἡ γλῶσσά μου) in the Psalm cited by Peter (Acts 2.26), which the early church read prophetically of Jesus, and demonstrates that the prophecy it contains was fulfilled in the ministry of Jesus.

Second, and more tentatively, I offer the following suggestion. Luke describes Jesus' prayer of thanksgiving in Lk. 10.21 with terms that imply speaking in tongues: inspired by the Spirit, Jesus bursts forth in exuberant and joyful praise, and this praise would have been understood by Luke's readers to include glossolalia. In this way, Luke presents Jesus' Spirit-inspired exultant praise and glossolalia as a model for his readers.

My third suggestion is closely related to the second. In view of the literary connections which tie the reference to 'my tongue rejoices' in Acts 2.26 together, on the one hand, with Jesus' Spirit-inspired exultation in Lk. 10.21 and, on the other hand, with the 'speaking in tongues' of Acts 2.4, 10.46, and 19.6, the reference to 'my tongue rejoices' suggests that Luke and the early church read this phrase from Ps. 16.9 as a reference to speaking in tongues, which they understood to have been practiced by Jesus. In other words, the early church viewed Jesus' experience of glossolalia (implied in Lk. 10.21) as a fulfillment of Ps. 16.9, which they read as a messianic prophecy. Just as the miraculous tongues of Jesus' disciples serve as proof of Jesus' resurrection and thus that he is Messiah and Lord (Acts 2.33), so also does Jesus' own experience of glossolalia serve as proof. It is the fulfillment of one aspect of the messianic prophecy contained in Ps. 16.8-11. This text (Ps. 16.9/Acts 2.26) also calls Luke's readers to see their own experience of tongues as further proof of Jesus' exalted status.

In addition to the literary connections noted above, these conclusions are supported by the manner in which Luke presents 'speaking in tongues' as the definitive and expected sign for reception of the Spirit of prophecy promised by Joel. This sign confirms that the disciples are the true people of God and also validates their proclamation that Jesus is Lord. Accordingly, a similar sign for the Messiah would be especially appropriate in Luke's scheme. These conclusions find further support in the positive and expectant attitude exemplified by Luke and his community toward speaking in tongues (e.g. Lk. 11.13). I have suggested that a messianic reading of Ps. 16.9 played an important role in the formation of this positive appraisal of tongues. Finally, I have also discussed possible historical reasons for the tentative nature of the evidence linking Jesus with speaking in tongues.

Application

Jesus' example reminds us that abundant, radiant, and overflowing joy should mark our worship services and our lives. Not long ago my wife and I visited our daughter and son-in-law who live in Omaha, Nebraska. That Sunday we attended Glad Tidings Assemblies of God, a vibrant and wonderfully diverse group of Christians. As the worship began, I immediately became strongly aware of God's presence and I was filled with an indescribable joy. The church was packed with many Africans, most of whom were wearing distinctive clothing from their respective regions of Africa. The group of worshippers also included a number of Hispanics and Asians as well as many Anglos and African-Americans. As I looked around, I was reminded of the scene from Revelation 7 where people from 'every nation, tribe, people, and language' gather before the throne of God and give praise to the Lamb. At one point I looked at the choir, who were erupting in song, dance, and praise and my eye caught the face of an Asian man with a huge smile and hands lifted in praise. Around him flowed a torrent of joy that was comprised of people who seemingly represented every nation under heaven. As I entered into this miraculous and spontaneous river of pure joy and intense devotion, I began to sense words welling up from within me. I was very much in control of my faculties and acutely aware of all that was taking place, but at the same time I was also swept up in joyful praise. The words flowed out and in a language that I did not understand. In that flood of joyful praise, I believe that only God and I heard the words that I uttered. Somehow, however, I sensed that my utterances were wonderfully connected with everything else taking place around me – it all issued from the same source. And the joy was palpable.

Reflection Questions

1. Luke presents Jesus' Spirit-inspired prophetic ministry, including his bold proclamation and exultant praise, as a model for us. Do you agree? What does this mean for you personally?

2. Menzies argues that Luke and the early church viewed Jesus' inspired and joyful praise recorded in Lk. 10.21 as a fulfillment of Ps. 16.9, which they read as a messianic prophecy. Does this make sense to you?

3. Menzies also argues that the language and logic of Luke's narrative point to the fact that Luke and the early church viewed Jesus' joyful praise (Lk. 10.21; cf. Acts 2.26) as including speaking in tongues. What are the implications for my prayer life and my patterns of worship?

4. Many Christians justify attitudes of indifference to or even open rejection of speaking in tongues in spite of the fact that this experience was modeled by the apostolic church. They do so by pointing to Jesus and saying, 'Well, if Jesus didn't speak in tongues, then this experience must not be very important for me?' How does the content of this chapter undercut this way of thinking?

4

JESUS, TONGUES, AND THE LONG ENDING OF MARK

In the previous chapter I argued that the literary connections and logic that tie the quotation from Ps. 16.9 (15.9, LXX), 'my tongue rejoices' (καὶ ἠγαλλιάσατο ἡ γλῶσσά μου), cited by Peter in Acts 2.26, together with the striking description of Jesus in Lk. 10.21, 'he rejoiced in the Holy Spirit' (ἠγαλλιάσατο ἐν τῷ πνεύματι τῷ ἁγίῳ) and multiple references to 'speaking in tongues' in Acts, suggest that Luke and his church understood Jesus' Spirit-inspired praise (Lk. 10.21) to include glossolalia, which they viewed as the fulfillment of one aspect of the messianic prophecy in Psalm 16. This thesis, and its corollary (i.e. that Jesus' prayer life was marked by glossolalia), are significantly strengthened if it can be demonstrated that the words attributed to Jesus in Mk 16.17, 'And these signs will accompany those who believe ... they will speak in new tongues' (σημεῖα δὲ τοῖς πιστεύσασιν ταῦτα παρακολουθήσει ... γλώσσαις λαλήσουσιν καιναῖς), are rooted in historically reliable tradition. Since this passage represents the only record of Jesus specifically referencing 'speaking in tongues', its significance for our understanding of Jesus' perspective on tongues and his spirituality can hardly be overestimated.

The fact that this saying of Jesus is found in the Gospel of Mark is proof enough for many that this record is historically reliable. Yet, the question is complicated by the fact that most contemporary scholars do not view the last 12 verses of Mark (Mk 16.9-20), often referred to as the long ending of Mark (LE), as a part of Mark's original Gospel. These verses were likely written by an unknown author in the early part of the second century (120-150 CE) and appended to the Gospel of Mark at this time.[1] Scholars are divided over how Mark's Gospel actually ended: some believe it originally ended at Mk 16.8; others feel that the original ending has been lost. However, there is widespread agreement that Mk 16.9-20 represents a later addition.[2]

The judgment that these verses probably do not stem from Mark's hand does not necessarily mean that these verses are not Scripture. Indeed, there are many reasons to acceptance these verses as canonical, even if one does not accept them as coming from Mark's hand. Virtually everything contained in the LE is found elsewhere in the New Testament; it was attached to Mark 'by the time final decisions were made about the limits to the NT canon',[3] and it was accepted by the Church as the Word of God without question for almost 1800 years. Yet, here again for our purposes we encounter a difficulty. Although, as we shall see, it is evident that virtually everything contained in the LE is found elsewhere in the New Testament, there are significant exceptions. These exceptions include the passage crucial to our central question cited above (Mk 16.17b) and the references to handling snakes and drinking poison that follow in Mk 16.18a:

> And these signs will accompany those who believe. In my name they will drive out demons; they will speak in new tongues; they will pick up snakes with their hands; and when they drink deadly poison, it will not hurt them at all; they will place their hands on sick people, and they will get well (Mk 16.17-18).

---

[1] James A. Kelhoffer, *Miracle and Mission: The Authentication of Missionaries and Their Message in the Longer Ending of Mark* (WUNT 2.112; Tübingen: Mohr Siebeck, 2000), p. 475.

[2] See Craig A. Evans, *Mark 8.27-16.20* (Word Biblical Commentary 34b; Nashville: Thomas Nelson Publishers, 2001), p. 545; N. Clayton Croy, *The Mutilation of Mark's Gospel* (Nashville: Abingdon Press, 2003), p. 14; Timothy J. Geddert, *Mark* (Believers Church Bible Commentary; Scottdale, PA: Herald Press, 2001), p. 403; C. Clifton Black, *Mark* (Abingdon NT Commentaries; Nashville: Abingdon Press, 2011), pp. 355-56; and Daniel Wallace, 'Mark 16.8 as the Conclusion to the Second Gospel', in David Alan Black (ed.), *Perspectives on the Ending of Mark* (Nashville: B&H Academic, 2008), pp. 1-39.

[3] Geddert, *Mark*, p. 403.

σημεῖα δὲ τοῖς πιστεύσασιν ταῦτα παρακολουθήσει. ἐν τῷ ὀνόματί μου δαιμόνια ἐκβαλοῦσιν, γλώσσαις λαλήσουσιν καιναῖς, καὶ ἐν ταῖς χερσὶν ὄφεις ἀροῦσιν κἂν θανάσιμόν τι πίωσιν οὐ μὴ αὐτοὺς βλάψῃ, ἐπὶ ἀρρώστους χεῖρας ἐπιθήσουσιν καὶ καλῶς ἕξουσιν (Mk 16.17-18).

So, how shall we view this saying of Jesus, particularly the words attributed to him in Mk 16.17b-18a?: '... they will speak in new tongues; they will pick up snakes with their hands; and when they drink deadly poison, it will not hurt them at all'. Do these words stem from historically reliable tradition? And if so, how shall we understand them? To these questions we now turn.

The Long Ending of Mark and Luke–Acts

As we have noted, most of the material found in the LE is paralleled in other portions of the New Testament, and, more specifically in the Gospels and Acts. James Kelhoffer argues that the author of the LE consciously drew from the Gospels and Acts, or at the very least, the underlying written traditions, when he or she composed this literary unit.[4] Kelhoffer specifically notes the strong connections between the LE and the Gospel of Luke. He concludes, 'With the exception of the LE's parallels to Mark 1.1-16.18, the most compelling evidence for literary dependence is to be found with the Gospel of Luke'.[5]

The points of connection between Mk 16.9-20 and Luke's narrative are particularly striking. Mark and Luke both highlight Mary Magdalene's role as a witness to the resurrection and note how the other disciples did not believe her testimony (Mk 16.11; Lk. 24.11).[6] Mark and Luke also refer to Jesus' post-resurrection encounter on the road with two disciples (Mk 16.12-13; Lk. 24.13-35).[7] Mark and Luke both emphasize the fact that the resurrected Jesus appeared to the eleven while they were eating and rebuked them for their lack of

---

[4] Kelhoffer, *Miracle*, pp. 131-47, 474.

[5] Kelhoffer, *Miracle*, p. 141.

[6] Only Mark and Luke describe Mary Magdalene as the one from whom Jesus cast out seven demons (Mk 16.9 and Lk. 8.2).

[7] Kelhoffer notes that after the brief introduction ('after these things'), 10 of 11 words in Mk 16.12 are found in Lk. 24.13-35 (*Miracle*, p. 144).

faith (Mk 16.14; Lk. 24.38-45). Mark and Luke both present Jesus' commissioning of the disciples for their future mission, which includes a reference to special 'signs' which will mark their ministry (Mk 16.15-20; Lk. 24.45-49 and Acts 1.4-8; 2.1-4,14-21).[8] Mark and Luke also describe Jesus' ascension to 'the right hand' of the Father (Mk 16.19; Lk. 24.51 and Acts 1.9-11; 2.33; 7.56). Finally, and particularly significant for our purposes, Mark and Luke specifically refer to speaking in tongues as one of the signs that will mark the disciples of Jesus (Mk 16.17; Acts 2.4, 15-21; 10.46; 19.6).

It should be noted that, apart from the reference to handling snakes and drinking poison in Mk 16.18, every point found in the LE finds significant parallels in Luke–Acts. Craig Evans outlines the connections between the LE and the other Gospels and Acts in the following manner:[9]

v. 11. Lack of belief (cf. Luke 24.11)

v. 12. Two on the road (cf. Luke 24.13-35)

v. 14. Reproach for unbelief (cf. John 20.19, 26)

v. 15. Great Commission (cf. Matt 28.19)

v. 16. Salvation/Judgment (cf. John 3.18, 36)

v. 17. Speaking in tongues (cf. Acts 2.4; 10.46)

v. 18. Serpents and poison (cf. Acts 28.3-5)

v. 19. Ascension (cf. Luke 24.51; Acts 1.2, 9)

v. 20. General summary of Acts

Evans' outline is instructive. However, it should also be noted that the verses from the LE that Evans connects to Matthean and Johannine parallels, also find significant counterparts in Luke's Gospel. Consider the following:

---

[8] As Hugh Anderson notes, 'The promise of charismatic gifts held out to those who believe indicates clearly enough that the narrator belonged to a community which held that speaking in tongues, exorcism, and healing were not confined to the Church's most primitive age but were the ongoing marks of authentic Christian faith' (*The Gospel of Mark* [New Century Bible Commentary; Grand Rapids: Eerdmans, 1976], p. 360). For a similar assessment, see R. Alan Cole, *The Gospel According to Mark: An Introduction and Commentary* (Tyndale NT Commentaries; Grand Rapids: Eerdmans, 2nd edn, 1989), p. 339.

[9] Evans, *Mark 8.27-16.20*, p. 546.

V. 14. *Reproach for unbelief.* As we have noted, Luke also highlights the fact that the resurrected Jesus appeared to the eleven while they were eating and rebuked them for their lack of faith (Lk. 24.38-45). Indeed, this theme connects the various stories contained in Luke 24. Here Jesus repeatedly rebukes the disciples for their lack of faith and their inability to understand the prophecies concerning himself (Lk. 24.6-8, 11, 25-27, 37-38, 44-49).[10]

V. 15. *Great Commission.* Luke also records Jesus' commission to his disciples in a similar fashion. In fact, Jesus' words of commission in Lk. 24.46 and Mk 16.15 begin in the same manner with the words, 'and he said to them' (καὶ εἶπεν αὐτοῖς). Both Luke and the author of the LE speak of 'preaching' (using forms of κηρύσσω; Mk 16.15; Lk. 24.47) to all nations or creation (Lk. 24.47: εἰς πάντα τὰ ἔθνη; Mk 16.15: πάσῃ τῇ κτίσει).[11]

V. 16. *Salvation/Judgment.* Water baptism as a response to repentance and faith is prominent in the book of Acts.[12] Unbelief (ἀπιστέω) is also highlighted in Luke's narrative, particularly in Lk. 24.11 and 24.41. The conclusion of Acts contains a note regarding the mixed response of those who heard Paul's preaching about Jesus: 'some were convinced ... but others would not believe' (Acts 28.24).

In view of the strong thematic and linguistic links that connect the LE with Luke–Acts, many of which are unique to these two writings (e.g. the description of Mary Magdalene; Jesus' post-resurrection encounter with two disciples; and various linguistic parallels), it would appear that the LE stems from a community significantly influenced by Luke's writings or, at the very least, by traditions utilized by Luke. Against the backdrop of this rich tapestry of interconnections, I would like to draw attention to a striking and unique theological affirmation that both Luke and the author of the LE make. Both Luke and the author of the LE present speaking in tongues as a positive, authenticating sign within and for the Chris-

---

[10] Kelhoffer also notes the striking way that Luke and the author of the LE use the phrase 'the rest' (τοῖς λοιποῖς; Lk. 24.9, Mk 16.13; see *Miracle*, p. 143).

[11] These similarities encouraged Kelhoffer to suggest that Mk 16.15-16 probably reflects a revision of Mt. 28.19 in light of Lk. 24.45-47 (*Miracle*, p. 145).

[12] See Acts 2.38, 41; 8.12-13, 36-38; 9.18; 10.47-48; 16.15, 33; 18.8; 19.5; 22.16.

tian community. This is particularly striking in that both Luke and the author of the LE present tongues as a sign not simply for the apostles or a select group of Christian leaders; but rather, they both present tongues as a sign available for each and every member of the Christian community.[13]

All of this suggests that the LE is grounded in solid, reliable, apostolic tradition. If we are reluctant to question the historical reliability of Luke–Acts, which has stood the test of historical scrutiny,[14] then we should pause before we too quickly reject or ignore material in the LE as inauthentic and irrelevant. Of course, there is still one question that demands an answer: How shall we understand and evaluate Jesus' words in Mk 16.18?

Making Sense of Snakes and Poison (Mark 16.18)

Mark 16.18, particularly the third and fourth signs cited by Jesus that 'will accompany those who believe', presents a problem for scholars and students of the Bible. First, it is hard to ignore the checkered history of interpretation that has led misguided souls to feature the handling of snakes, which in turn has resulted in tragedy and reproach for the church. Additionally, unlike so much of the other material in the LE, we find no parallels for these signs in the rest of the New Testament. Many commentators seek to illuminate the reference to the handling of snakes in Mk 16.18 by pointing to Acts 28.3-5, where we read that Paul, bitten by a viper, shakes the creature off into a fire and remains unharmed.[15] Yet this interpretative approach is fraught with difficulties. As Kelhoffer notes,

---

[13] Contra James A. Kelhoffer, who notes the connections between Mk 16.9-20 and Luke–Acts, but claims that only the LE presents tongues as an ongoing sign for believers beyond the apostles (*Miracle*, pp. 141-47, 281). I argue that this perspective is also shared by Luke in Robert Menzies, 'The Sending of the Seventy', pp. 87-113. In this regard, see also Menzies, *Pentecost* and its devotional companion volume, Robert Menzies, *Making Pentecost Your Story: 50 Days of Reflection and Prayer* (Xanesti eBook, 2015).

[14] See I. Howard Marshall, *Luke: Historian and Theologian* (Carlisle, UK: Paternoster, 1988), William M. Ramsay, *St. Paul the Traveller and Roman Citizen* (ed. Mark Wilson; Grand Rapids: Kregel, 2001 [orig. 1895]) and, more generally on the gospels, Craig L. Blomberg, *The Historical Reliability of the Gospels* (Downers Grove, IL: InterVarsity Press, 2nd edn, 2007).

[15] Note that the term for 'viper' in Acts 28.3 is ἔχιδνα, which implies a poisonous variety of snake, while Mk 16.18 uses the more generic ὄφις for 'snake'.

If someone were to argue that the LE's third sign is derived exclusively from Acts 28, it would have to be inferred that the author of the LE has transformed a single, inadvertent experience of Paul into a regular, deliberate practice of Jesus' followers. Although possible, this is unlikely and, in light of the many other pieces of evidence discussed in this chapter, methodologically short-sighted.[16]

Scholars also generally draw a complete blank when trying to find a suitable backdrop for Jesus' reference to 'drinking deadly poison'.[17] Some point to early Christian accounts of believers being forced to drink poison and surviving, but virtually all of these are later than the LE and provide, at best, very loose illustrations. It should not surprise us, then, that Kelhoffer, after his exhaustive study of Greco-Roman, Jewish, and Christian sources, concludes, '... the ultimate origin of the signs involving snakes and poison lies beyond a simple explanation'.[18] After almost 500 pages of detailed analysis, Kelhoffer is unable to explain the origin or meaning of this problematic saying of Jesus. Of course, he is not alone. The entire field of Markan scholars has either ignored this text, treated it with disdain and indifference, or simply given up. It is a riddle that seemingly defies explanation. However, I would like to propose a solution to this vexing puzzle. It is a solution that seeks to understand this saying as a creative application of a text from the Old Testament: Job 20.16. To this passage we now turn.

---

[16] Kelhoffer, *Miracle*, p. 402. On the issue of handling snakes, Kelhoffer concludes: '[T]here is no direct parallel to Mark 16.18a in ancient Jewish or Christian writings' (*Miracle*, p. 407).

[17] An exception is found in James R. Edwards, *The Gospel According to Mark* (Pillar NT Commentary; Grand Rapids: Eerdmans, 2002), pp. 506-507. Edwards suggests that 'in the late first century a cult related to poisonous drugs was exerting at least some influence' and points to Josephus and tentatively Ignatius to support this claim. Adela Yarbro Collins also offers a good summary of various accounts of drinking poison (*Mark: A Commentary* [Hermeneia; Minneapolis: Fortress Press, 2007], pp. 814-15). Nevertheless, as Kelhoffer notes, none of these texts can account for the origin of this saying (*Miracle*, p. 470).

[18] Kelhoffer, *Miracle*, p. 478. Again, with reference to drinking poison, Kelhoffer states, '... the origin of this statement concerning the drinking of a deadly substance [Mark 16.18a] cannot be reduced to a single source or precedent, either literary or historical' (*Miracle*, p. 470).

Job 20.16 as the Interpretative Key to Mark 16.18

In Job 20.16 we read of the ill-timed, if not entirely inaccurate, counsel of one of Job's 'comforters', Zophar the Naamathite. Zophar describes the sad lot in life of the wicked and godless (Job 20.5). Zophar's oracle of doom reaches a crescendo in Job 20.16 as he describes the terrible fate that awaits the unrighteous:

'He will suck the poison of serpents;
the fangs of an adder will kill him'.

The LXX of Job 20.16 and my literal translation read as follows:

Θυμὸν δὲ δρακόντων θηλάσειεν
ἀνέλοι δὲ αὐτὸν γλῶσσα ὄφεως

The anger of dragons (or serpents) he shall suck,
the tongue of the snake shall destroy him.

The Hebrew text of Job 20.16 and my literal translation follow as well:

ראש־פתנים יינק תהרגהו לשון אפעה:

The head of serpents he shall suck,
the tongue (*lashon*) of the viper shall slay him.

There is a parallel, poetic structure in the Hebrew version of this saying. The 'head of serpents' in the first stich parallels 'the tongue of the viper' in the second. In the first stich of the verse, the unrighteous person is pictured as 'sucking' the head of the serpents, a clear allusion to drinking the venom of the snake. This picture is clarified further by the context (cf. Job 20.13-15), especially Job 20.14, which speaks of 'the venom of serpents' within the stomach of the wicked. The second stich, 'the tongue of the viper shall slay him', again utilizes vivid imagery. The meaning is transparent, for 'the tongue of the viper' clearly refers to the bite of the viper, which will kill.

   Here, then, we have a single text from the Old Testament that offers in a concise and vivid manner parallels to both of the problematic sayings of Jesus found in Mk 16.18: 'the head of serpents he shall suck' accounts for 'when they drink deadly poison, it will not hurt them' and 'the tongue of the viper shall slay him' corresponds to 'they will pick up snakes with their hands' (with the implication that they will not be harmed). Of course, in the context of the LE,

Jesus has taken this saying from Job and applied it in a fresh way with new meaning. Whereas in Job, this passage refers to the judgment that will come upon the godless; in the teaching of Jesus this oracle of doom has been reversed. The disciples of Jesus will not experience the terrible fate that is the lot of the wicked; rather, Jesus' disciples will be protected from these calamities.

We have already highlighted how the material in Mk 16.9-20 is largely drawn from either Luke's Gospel or traditions utilized by Luke. Here again Luke's Gospel provides a fitting context for understanding more specifically the meaning of these sayings of Jesus. In Luke's Gospel the image of the snake represents satanic influence or opposition. Lk. 11.11-12 is a case in point, 'Which of you fathers, if your son asks for a fish, will give him a snake instead? Or if he asks for an egg, will give him a scorpion?' Here the snake and the scorpion refer to dangerous gifts. It should be noted that Luke's comparisons feature dangerous objects ('snake' and 'scorpion'), whereas in the parallel passage in Matthew's Gospel, Matthew's comparisons include one that is simply useless ('stone' and 'snake', Mt. 7.9-10). This suggests that Luke was consciously seeking to help his readers overcome their fear. These harmful gifts are contrasted with the gift of the Spirit that our Heavenly Father delights to give us. In view of the Beelzebub controversy (Lk. 11.14-26) that immediately follows, the metaphors of the snake and scorpion should be seen as representing dangerous, satanic power, which is contrasted with the power of the Holy Spirit. Luke highlights that we need not fear, for the Father only gives good gifts (i.e. the Holy Spirit)!

In Lk. 10.18-19 the snake and scorpion metaphors appear once again. The seventy(-two) return with joy from their mission. Jesus declares,

> I saw Satan fall like lightning from heaven. I have given you authority to trample on snakes and scorpions and to overcome all the power of the enemy; nothing will harm you (Lk. 10.18-19).

Here the demonic character of the snake and scorpion metaphor is explicitly stated. The fact that the snake is again paired with the scorpion is not coincidental. A number of recent scholarly studies have noted that in his Travel Narrative, Luke 'presents Jesus as the prophet like Moses, on a journey to Jerusalem to effect a new Exodus for the people of God'.[19] One need not accept in its entirety the theses of C.F. Evans or David Moessner, both of whom suggest that Luke structures his Travel Narrative largely on the basis of the book of Deuteronomy, to recognize that an interest in Moses typology has influenced Luke's literary program in a significant way.[20] Certainly we should not miss the fact that the words 'serpent' (ὄφις) and 'scorpion' (σκορπίος) which appear together in Lk. 10.19 are found together in the Old Testament (LXX) only in Deut. 8.15: 'He led you through the vast and dreadful desert, that thirsty and waterless land, with its venomous snakes and scorpions'. Thus, we see that the metaphor of the snake, rooted as it is in the Exodus story, represents satanic influence and opposition.

Luke 10.19, then, together with Job 20.16, sheds significant light on the sayings of Jesus recorded in Mk 16.18. It represents a close parallel, a sort of commentary, on Jesus' words: 'They will pick up snakes with their hands; and when they drink deadly poison, it will not hurt them at all' is another way of saying that the disciples of Jesus will overcome satanic opposition and persecution.[21] The curse of Job 20.16 is reversed. The venom of the viper and the bite of the snake will have no impact.

Jewish Exegesis and the Significance of Job 20.16

It is significant that the Hebrew text of Job 20.16 refers to 'the tongue (*lashon*) of the viper'. In Mk 16.17-18, when Jesus speaks of the signs that will follow those who believe, he lists in order: the casting out of demons, speaking in tongues, handling snakes, drinking poison, and healing the sick. It is indeed striking that the signs of handling snakes and drinking poison follow immediately after the

---

[19] Greg W. Forbes, *The God of Old: The Role of the Lukan Parables in the Purpose of Luke's Gospel* (JSNTSS 198; Sheffield: Sheffield Academic Press, 2000), p. 329.

[20] So also Edward J. Woods, *The 'Finger of God' and Pneumatology in Luke–Acts* (JSNTSS 205; Sheffield: Sheffield Academic Press, 2001), pp. 47-48. Note also C.F. Evans, 'The Central Section of Luke's Gospel', in D.E. Nineham (ed.), *Studies in the Gospels* (Oxford: Blackwell, 1957), pp. 37-53 and David P. Moessner, *Lord of the Banquet: The Literary and Theological Significance of the Lukan Travel Narrative* (Minneapolis: Fortress Press, 1989).

[21] It should be noted that Washingtoniensis, a fourth or fifth century manuscript, includes an extended saying between Mk 16.14 and 16.15. This 'Freer Logion' has the disciples 'citing Satanic oppression as an excuse for their faithlessness in abandoning Jesus' (Joel Marcus, *Mark 8-16* [The Anchor Yale Bible 27A; New Haven, CT: Yale University Press, 2009], p. 1090).

sign of tongues. Once it is understood that Jesus originally drew upon the Hebrew text of Job 20.16 when he uttered this saying, the order of the signs makes perfect sense. The order of the signs in Mk 16.17-18 reflects the *Stichwort* connection (common in Jewish interpretation) between the believers' 'new *tongues*' and the following sign of 'handling snakes', which draws upon the '*tongue* of a snake' in Job 20.16. In other words, the *Stichwort* connection that hinges on the term 'tongue' explains why the signs from Job 20.16, handling snakes and drinking poison, follow the reference to 'new tongues' in the list of signs in Mk 16.17-18.

This insight not only bolsters the case for seeing Job 20.16 as the OT inspiration for Jesus' words in Mk 16.18, it also represents a strong argument that this saying stems from Jesus himself. The Jewish character of this rhetorical device or hermeneutical method is evident. Richard Longenecker identifies this midrashic method of interpretation, which connects two verses by the use of a common term or *Stichwort*, as a form of *gezerah shavah*.[22] Of course, this *Stichwort* connection is not evident in the Greek text of Mark's Gospel. Mark's Gospel thus represents a later stage in the transmission of this tradition, one that offers a translation of the Semitic original, which is rooted in the Hebrew text of Job 20.16. The very Jewish nature of this saying, evidenced by the allusions to Job 20.16 and the *Stichwort* ordering of the sequence of signs, suggests that this saying stems from Jesus himself.

The evidence thus indicates that there were two significant steps in the development and transmission of the tradition passed on in Mk 16.17-18. The first step takes us back to Jesus. Jesus, speaking of the signs that will mark his disciples, refers to the 'new tongues' (glossolalia) that they will speak; and then, utilizing symbolic imagery from Job 20.16 (i.e. the venom and 'tongue' or bite of the viper), notes that they will be protected from and overcome satanic opposition (cf. Lk. 10.18-19). The references to 'tongue' link these specifics signs together in the list that Jesus gives.

The second step is found in the translation of this saying of Jesus into Greek.[23] The author of the LE passes this saying on, draw-

<hr/>

[22] Richard N. Longenecker, *Biblical Exegesis in the Apostolic Period* (Grand Rapids: Eerdmans, 2nd edn, 1999), p. 20.

[23] Note that Maurice Casey claims to 'have found substantial and decisive evidence that parts of Mark's Gospel are literal translations of written Aramaic

ing upon the LXX of Job 20.16,[24] but in a loosely paraphrased form that does not highlight the *Stichwort* connection of the term 'tongue'. In Luke's Gospel references to 'snakes (and scorpions)' are rooted in the Exodus tradition and this association appears to have become more prominent with the passage of time. Nevertheless, only the text of Job 20.16 adequately explains the origins of this saying, with its reference to protection from drinking deadly poison and the potential dangers of snakes. This text also explains the association and order of these signs in Jesus' list as it appears in the LE.

The History of a Tradition: Mark 16.17-18

Kelhoffer notes that Eusebius of Caesarea (260-340 CE) and Philip of Side (active in 434-439 CE) pass on traditions about Justus Barsabbas drinking poison. These traditions originate with Papias of Hierapolis, whose writings were produced in the early part of the second century.[25] The tradition states that Justus was 'tested by unbelievers' (δοκιμαζόμενος) and thus forced 'to drink viper's venom' (ἰὸν ἐχίδνης πιών). He was protected by the name of Christ from harm (ἀπαθὴς διεφυλάχθη). However, Kelhoffer notes 'one discrepancy' between Philip's account and that of Eusebius. Philip writes that Justus drank 'viper's venom' (ἰὸν ἐχίδνης), whereas Eusebius simply states that Justus drank a 'harmful drug' (δηλητήριον φάρμακον; *Hist. eccl.* 3.39).[26]

Kelhoffer goes on to argue that Philip's later account, at least on the issue of Justus' drink, preserves Papias' account more faithfully.[27] Kelhoffer argues that Eusebius was probably aware of the fact that 'a snake's venom is not harmful if imbibed, but rather *only* if it

---

sources' (Casey, *Aramaic Sources of Mark's Gospel* [SNTS 102; Cambridge: University Press, 1998], p. 254).

[24] The LXX of Job 20.16 and the LE (Mk 16.18) use the term, ὄφις, to refer to the snake.

[25] Kelhoffer, *Miracle*, p. 433.

[26] See Philippus Sidetes, frag. 6, citing or paraphrasing Papias of Hierapolis, *Explanation of the Lord's Sentences*: Greek text. Carl de Boor, *Neue Fragmente des Papias, Hegesippus und Pierius, in bischer unbekannten Excerpten aus der Kirchengeschichte des Philippus Sidetes* (TU 5.2; Leipzig: J.C. Hinrich, 1888), pp. 165-84 (p. 170 for this fragment). These texts are cited in Kelhoffer, *Miracle*, pp. 437-38.

[27] Kelhoffer, *Miracle*, pp. 433-42.

enters directly into a person's blood stream'.[28] Thus, aware of a potential problem in the original version, Eusebius altered Papias' account by giving a more general description of the poison. Kelhoffer also notes that the movement from a specific description to a more general one is characteristic of later editorial work.[29]

I found Kelhoffer's analysis of how Philip of Side and Eusebius of Caesarea passed on Papias' tradition of Justus drinking 'viper's venom' particularly interesting. My interest was piqued because the arguments that Kelhoffer advances for the primacy or authenticity of Philip's account over against that passed on by Eusebius could also be applied to the tradition history of Mk 16.17-18 that I am proposing. Jesus' reference to the 'viper's venom' of Job 20.16 might well have been rendered in a less specific way as it was translated into Greek (i.e. transformed from 'the tongue of the viper' to picking 'up snakes with their hands' and from drinking 'the venom of vipers' to drinking 'deadly poison'). The same factors that Kelhoffer suggests influenced Eusebius to write a more general summary might well have encouraged the scribes who penned the Greek account utilized by the author of the LE to write a more streamlined, less specific, and, perhaps according to their sensibilities, a more coherent, account as well.[30]

Conclusion

I have argued that the author of the LE draws heavily from Luke–Acts or, at the very least, from traditions utilized by Luke. This influence extends to Mk 16.17-18, which refers to speaking in tongues, and protection from snakes and deadly poison as signs that will mark the disciples of Jesus. Luke not only describes speaking in tongues as a sign that is available to every believer, his use of 'snakes and scorpions' as metaphors for satanic opposition and persecution (Lk. 10.18-19; 11.11-13) shed valuable light on Jesus' words in Mk 16.18.

---

[28] Kelhoffer, *Miracle*, p. 438, italics his.

[29] Kelhoffer, *Miracle*, p. 438.

[30] It might also be argued that Papias' description of Justus' ordeal (as recorded by Philip of Side) was influenced by Jesus' rhetorical use of Job 20.16, both of which speak of drinking 'the venom of vipers'.

More specifically, however, I have argued that Jesus' words in Mk 16.18 draw upon Job 20.16. Against this OT backdrop these signs (Mk 16.18) signify that believers, as a general rule, will be protected from harm, especially persecution, as they engage in their mission. While the unrighteous person in Job's narrative will 'suck the venom of vipers' and be 'killed by the tongue of a snake', the followers of Jesus will be protected from these perils, which symbolize satanic opposition and persecution (Lk. 10.18-19).

I also noted that the order of the signs found in Mk 16.17-18 is influenced by the *Stichwort* connection between the believers' 'new *tongues*' and the following sign of 'handling snakes', which draws upon the '*tongue* of a snake' in Job 20.16. This Jewish hermeneutical method, then, explains why the signs from Job 20.16, handling snakes and drinking poison, follow the reference to 'new tongues' in Jesus' list of signs.

The Jewish nature of this rhetorical device suggests that this saying (Mk 16.17-18) stems from Jesus himself. The evidence suggests that there were two stages in the development of the tradition passed on in Mk 16.17-18.

First, Jesus, speaking of the signs that will mark his disciples, refers to the 'new tongues' (glossolalia) that they will speak; and then, utilizing symbolic imagery from Job 20.16 (i.e. the poison and 'tongue' or bite of a snake), notes that his disciples will be protected from and overcome satanic opposition (cf. Lk. 10.18-19). The references to 'tongue' link these specifics signs together in Jesus' list of signs.

In the second and later stage, the author of the LE passes on this saying of Jesus, now translated into Greek, by drawing upon the LXX of Job 20.16, but in a loosely paraphrased and generalized form that does not highlight the *Stichwort* connection of the term 'tongue'. In the Gospel of Luke the references to 'snakes (and scorpions)' are rooted in the Exodus tradition and these associations become more prominent with the passage of time. Nevertheless, in spite of this generalizing tendency – a process illustrated in the manner in which Philip of Side and Eusebius of Caesarea pass on Papias' tradition of Justus drinking 'viper's venom' – it is evident that only the text of Job 20.16 adequately explains the origin of this saying, with its reference to protection from drinking deadly poison and the potential dangers of snakes.

An important corollary emerges from these conclusions. I have argued that the LE is grounded in reliable, apostolic tradition. This historically reliable tradition includes the words of Jesus recorded in Mk 16.17-18. Jesus himself describes tongues as a sign available for each and every disciple.

Application

Some people look down upon talk of 'signs'. They feel that this is somehow unspiritual or beneath them. Perhaps they have in mind Jesus' rebuke of those who sought 'a miraculous sign' (Lk. 11.29). Yet these 'sign seekers' were looking for the wrong kind of messiah and so also the wrong kind of sign. Thus, they failed to recognize that Jesus was the Messiah whom they sought. In any event, however we understand this passage, it should be noted that these cautionary words simply give perspective to the positive emphasis on 'signs and wonders' found elsewhere in Scripture.[31]

The church in China has not shied away from emphasizing God's miraculous 'signs and wonders'. In March of 2014 I met with several leaders of a large, Pentecostal house church network. The Li Xin (*Zhong Hua Meng Fu* or China Is Blessed) Church was established in the early 1980s in Anhui Province. It has grown rapidly over the past 20 years and now has churches all over China. The founder and leader of the church, Uncle Zheng, shared with me his fascinating story.

Uncle Zheng indicated that in the early days (1980s) the church was like the church in the book of Acts. They relied heavily on testimonies, miracles of healing, and the casting out of demons. And the church grew rapidly. He told of one lady who was baptized in a river near the church. She took a bottle with her and filled it with 'holy water' from the river when she was baptized. She then took this water back to her husband, who was very sick, and told him to drink it. He did and was wonderfully healed. Zheng and the others said that they had many stories like this.

An important event took place in 1983. The police were pressuring Zheng to stop his church meetings and close down the church.

---

[31] For 'signs and wonders', see Acts 2.19, 22, 43; 4.30; 5.12; 6.8; 7.36; 14.3; 15.12. Note also Mark's positive reference to 'signs' in Mk 16.17.

Finally, he said that he would, but that he wanted to meet with the believers one last time. When he returned home, his mother, who at this time was possessed by a demon, began to laugh in a loud, demonic voice. When Zheng heard this demonic laugh, which seemed to symbolize Satan's triumph, he felt prompted by the Holy Spirit not to give up and close down the church. Zheng indicated that this was the beginning of a period of many miracles and rapid growth in the church. Zheng's mother was also wonderfully converted and freed from satanic bondage.

The Pentecostal message, complete with an emphasis on speaking in tongues, came to the church in 1988. Two Christian brothers were released from prison after spending 15 years in a labor camp. Zheng noted that the earlier generation (1950s to 70s) of evangelists spent many years in labor camps; his generation (1980s and 90s) represented the 'short-term' generation, because they only spent a few years in prison. These two brothers encouraged Zheng and his church to consider the role of speaking in tongues in their own worship and prayer lives. They also introduced them to a Romanian missionary, Brother Matthew, who brought to them the Pentecostal message of tongues as the sign of baptism in the Holy Spirit. They said from this point on, they began to emphasize the work of the Spirit and speaking in tongues.

The church began to grow rapidly and spread beyond the borders of Anhui Province beginning in 1990. A catalyst for this came in 1993. The police attempted to arrest Zheng and their efforts forced him into an itinerant mode of ministry. From 1993 through 2002 he traveled widely through many provinces, preaching and evading the police. Although Zheng stated that their church does not face strong opposition or persecution now, this earlier period was an important time of church growth, stimulated by persecution. He noted that this was also the experience of the early church in Acts.

I asked Zheng and the other leaders how they would compare the church today with the church of the earlier years (1980s). They said that the church of the early years was largely a village church and that the gospel moved from the villages to the cities. Now, they said that the church is taking root in the cities and the gospel is now moving from the cities to the villages. They feel that this transformation of the church from a largely rural context to a predominately urban setting is a part of God's plan. They noted the parallels with the growth of the church in the book of Acts: the church began with uneducated fishermen like Peter; but, as it expanded into the Gentile world, God used an educated man like Paul to help the church expand. So also in China, God used illiterate villagers to establish the church; now he is using university graduates to take the gospel to those in the cities and beyond. Their church now emphasizes planting churches among the university students of the cities because they see this as the future of China's church.

Zheng viewed the early days, when they did not have a Bible and people experienced miracles in a way that might be viewed as superstitious, in a positive way. He noted that in those days, 'We did not begin our presentation of the gospel by talking about sin and the need for forgiveness'. These were concepts that the villagers would not readily understand or feel significant. Rather, they began by talking about Jesus' power to heal and to free people from demonic bondage. In time, people came to understand other elements and implications of the gospel, but this was God's way of reaching down and touching people at their point of need. I found this striking, for it reminded me of the ministry of Jesus. Zheng and his colleagues did not view the focus on the miraculous as superstitious; rather, they understood these experiences as God graciously accommodating his work to their situation and needs – a divinely inspired contextualization of the gospel.

I expected that they might say that today in the urban centers their approach is quite different. But actually, they did not. When I asked if they continue to emphasize praying for the sick and casting out demons today, they looked at me with faces filled with bewilderment. How else would you present the good news of Jesus? Even though the cognitive aspect of their message is undoubtedly more pronounced when communicating with the university students than with the villagers, they still maintain a strong emphasis on the reality of God's power and encountering Him in a personal and tangible way.

Thus, it is not surprising that Zheng and the others have a favorable view of the church today. They highlighted that their churches continue to emphasize and experience the Holy Spirit's power and gifts, such as speaking in tongues. Zheng put it this way: 'While we believe that the apostles are gone [limited to the Twelve]; the Spirit of the apostles is still the same'. He also said that, 'Acts is the pattern for the mission of the church. If the church does not follow the path of the early church, we will lose our way.'

Zheng's comments raise for us an important question. Which path are we following?

Reflection Questions

1. Have you ever considered whether or not we should view Mk 16.9-20 as part of the inspired word of God? Menzies suggests that even though these verses originally were not a part of the Gospel of Mark, they should be considered a part of the Bible. Why?

2. Menzies offers a fresh way of reading Mk 16.17-18, the description of the signs that Jesus says will mark his followers. Do you feel that his interpretation of these verses makes sense? What does this mean for you?

3. If Menzies is correct, Jesus declared that speaking in tongues is one of the signs that will mark his followers. This should not surprise us, for tongues reminds us of our connection to the apostolic church and of the fact that we too share their calling to be witnesses for Jesus. Do you find this to be the case in your life? If not, why not?

4. Do you see how Jesus' words in Mk 16.17 lend support to the author's reading of Lk. 10.21? What does this say to us about Jesus' prayer life? What does it suggest about our prayer life?

PART THREE

PAUL AND TONGUES

INTRODUCTION

Our study of Luke–Acts and the Gospel of Mark has revealed that for Christians speaking in tongues serves as a dramatic, observable sign of God's powerful presence in our midst and his call upon our lives. In Chapter 7 we shall argue that in addition to serving as a sign, speaking in tongues also functions as a form of Spirit-inspired prayer and, in special instances in the corporate setting, as a means of proclamation. However, we shall begin our inquiry into Paul's assessment of speaking in tongues in Chapter 5 by first addressing the question, Does Paul view speaking in tongues as a gift that is available and desirable for every believer? In Chapter 6 we shall then seek to answer another important question, How do we reconcile Luke's presentation of speaking in tongues as a positive sign with Paul's apparently disparaging comments about tongues as a negative sign in 1 Cor. 14.20-25?

Let us now turn to Paul and his attitude toward speaking in tongues. Although we shall see that Paul's words of instruction regarding tongues are not limited to 1 Corinthians 12-14, any discussion of the gift of tongues must treat in considerable detail this important passage.

5

PAUL:
TONGUES FOR EVERY BELIEVER

In 1 Corinthians 12-14 Paul refers to glossolalia (tongues) as one of the gifts God grants to the church. A thorough reading of these chapters reveals that, in spite of the Corinthian's misunderstanding and abuse of this gift, Paul holds the private manifestation of tongues in high regard.[1] Although Paul is concerned to direct the Corinthians towards a more mature expression of spiritual gifts 'in the assembly' – and thus he focuses on the need for edification and the primacy of prophecy over uninterpreted tongues in the corporate setting – Paul never denigrates the gift of tongues. Indeed, Paul affirms that the private manifestation of tongues is edifying to the speaker (1 Cor. 14.4) and, in an autobiographical note, he thanks God for the frequent manifestation of tongues in his private prayer-life (1 Cor. 14.18). Fearful that his instructions to the Corinthians concerning the proper use of tongues 'in the assembly' might be misunderstood, he explicitly commands them not to forbid speaking in tongues (1 Cor. 14.39). And, with reference to the private manifestation of tongues, Paul declares, 'I would like every one of you to speak in tongues …' (1 Cor. 14.5).

Paul's words at this point, particularly the wish expressed in 1 Cor. 14.5, have led many to conclude that Paul viewed the private manifestation of tongues as edifying and available to every believer. As a result, most Pentecostals and many Charismatics believe and

---

[1] So also Gordon D. Fee, *The First Epistle to the Corinthians* (NICNT; Grand Rapids: Eerdmans, 1987), p. 659.

teach that every believer can be strengthened through the manifestation of tongues during times of private prayer. This conclusion and reading of Paul have been challenged in a thoughtful and engaging article by Max Turner.[2] In my opinion, Turner's article, irenic in tone and addressed to those in the Pentecostal community, serves to stimulate exactly the kind of dialogue that we in the Christian community need. Turner's article and the ensuing responses will undoubtedly help us all better understand each other, our points of commonality, and why we may choose to differ on certain points. This sort of dialogue also challenges all of us to reexamine our positions in light of the Scriptures. Although this process will not always result in agreement, I believe that it will serve to build a sense of unity and mutual respect within the body of Christ. Ultimately, it will help us reflect more faithfully the mind of Christ. It is with this hope that I offer the following response to Turner's article, my attempt to contribute to this dialogue. Three major issues will be treated: first, the nature of the problem Paul addresses in 1 Corinthians 12-14 and its implications for our question concerning the potential universality of tongues; second, the force of the rhetorical question in 1 Cor. 12.30b, 'Do all speak in tongues?'; and third, the significance of Paul's wishful declaration in 1 Cor. 14.5, 'I would like everyone of you to speak in tongues ...' I will conclude by responding to Turner's probing questions concerning the present shape of Pentecostal theology, especially his critique of the doctrine of initial evidence.

The Problem at Corinth

Turner notes that 1 Corinthians 12-14 is polemical. Here Paul is attempting to correct problems in the Corinthians' understanding and use of tongues. At least some of the Corinthians appear to have viewed tongues as an expression of a superior level of spirituality. Thus, they valued tongues above other gifts and, in the context of corporate meetings, their spiritual elitism often found expression in unintelligible outbursts that disrupted meetings and did not build up

---

[2] Max Turner, 'Tongues: An Experience for All in the Pauline Churches?', *Asian Journal of Pentecostal Studies* 1 (1998), pp. 231-53.

the church.[3] This basic reconstruction of the problem at Corinth has found widespread acceptance. However, as Turner notes, one matter is less clear. Were all of the Corinthians caught up in this elitist form of spirituality (and thus standing in opposition to Paul) or was the church itself divided over the issue? The former position has been advocated by Fee, the latter by Forbes.[4]

Turner himself opts for the latter position, following closely the lead of Forbes. Thus he suggests that at Corinth the gift of tongues was exercised by some to establish or reinforce their position as a member of the spiritual elite. The exercise of tongues was, then, a part of the 'power games' that divided the church at Corinth. Turner suggests that this in turn indicates that the exercise of tongues at Corinth 'was a relatively restricted phenomenon'.[5] He reasons, 'if all or most could speak in tongues – if only as private prayer and doxology – then manifestation of the gift could provide no grounds for elitist claims'.[6]

Yet Turner's reasoning here seems to miss a vital point: the central question is not whether or not all of the Corinthians *actually* spoke in tongues; but rather, did Paul teach or imply that this was potentially the case? Here it is worthwhile to note that if Turner's reconstruction of the problem is accurate – that is, that an elitist group was disrupting meetings with outbursts of tongues because they felt this marked them off as part of a super-spiritual group – then Paul's references to the potentially universal character of tongues as an edifying dimension of one's private prayer-life is readily explicable. An analysis of Paul's argument is instructive in this regard.

Paul seeks to correct the Corinthians' misunderstanding: he highlights the variety and origin of God's gracious gifts (1 Corinthians 12, esp. vv. 4-6), that everyone has a role to play (1 Cor. 12.11-27), and that edification is the key goal (1 Cor. 12.7). Specifically, with reference to tongues, he insists that in the assembly, unless tongues are interpreted, they do not edify the church and thus

---

[3] Turner, 'Experience for All', pp. 235-36.

[4] Fee, *First Corinthians*, pp. 4-15; Christopher Forbes, *Prophecy and Inspired Speech in Early Christianity and its Hellenistic Environment* (Tübingen: Mohr, 1995), pp. 14-16, 171-75, 182-87, 260-64.

[5] Turner, 'Experience for All', p. 237.

[6] Turner, 'Experience for All', p. 237.

prophecy is to be preferred (1 Cor. 14.2-5). In the context of his argument that prophecy is greater than tongues in the assembly, Paul also states that the private manifestation of tongues is edifying to the speaker and, furthermore, that it is not limited to an elite group, but rather available to all (1 Cor. 14.5, 18). In other words, just as Paul notes that he is no stranger to tongues and thus qualified to speak of the gift's significance (perhaps here he bests the Corinthians at their own game of elitist claims; 14.18), so also Paul undermines the Corinthians' sense of superiority with his comments concerning the universality of the gift. If Turner's reconstruction of the problem is correct, this then may indeed be the thrust of 14.5. All can be edified by the private manifestation of tongues (this is not reserved to a select group), but in the assembly it is more spiritual to prophesy (since this is intelligible and edifying).

In short, Turner's reconstruction of the problem does not indicate that Paul viewed the gift of tongues as limited to a select group within the church. In fact, it is quite the opposite. Turner's reconstruction actually offers a positive reason for Paul to affirm the universality of tongues. In the face of elitist claims, we can understand Paul's words in 14.5 ('I would like every one of you to speak in tongues …') as a subtle corrective. While Turner's reconstruction might suggest that only members of the problem group at Corinth actually spoke in tongues, this is by no means necessarily the case. On the one hand, as Fee suggests, it is quite possible that we should see the entire church standing in opposition to Paul. If this is the case, then tongues might have been widely exercised by the entire church. On the other hand, even if the problem was localized in a group within the church, it is still quite likely that the private manifestation of tongues was not limited to this select group. The key problem at Corinth with reference to tongues was the abuse of the gift 'in the assembly' (that is, when the church gathered together; cf. 1 Cor. 12.28; 14.4-6, 9-19). It is certainly possible to envision the elitist group reveling in their *public display* of tongues, regardless of whether or not there were others who exercised the gift in private such as Paul (1 Cor. 14.18).[7] This public display of 'speaking mysteries' (14.2) would be sign enough of their special knowledge and po-

---

[7] The contrast between 1 Cor. 14.18 ('I thank God I speak in tongues more than you all') and 14.19 ('But, in the church …') indicates that Paul's autobiographical comments in 14.18 refer to the private exercise of tongues.

sition, superior to any private usage. Of course, with this flawed thinking, Paul cannot agree. In this case, Paul's words in 1 Cor. 14.5 would serve to remind the elitist group of the larger reality reflected in their midst (of which, they may or may not have been aware): all can be edified through the private manifestation of the gift.

Paul's Rhetorical Question (1 Corinthians 12.30b)

Turner next moves to the rhetorical question in 1 Cor. 12.30b, 'Do all speak in tongues?' As the Greek grammar indicates, the anticipated answer is 'No'. For those not wishing to deal with the complexities of Paul's argument, this statement is often taken as the final word on this issue. However, Paul's treatment of tongues in 1 Corinthians 14 warns us against making such a premature judgment. Upon closer analysis we see that Paul here is clearly dealing with the exercise of gifts 'in the assembly' (1 Cor. 12.28). In other words, when Paul asks, 'Do all speak in tongues?', he is not asking, 'Can all speak in tongues (in private or corporate contexts)?' Rather, he is making a point very much in line with what precedes in chapter 12: when we gather together, not everyone contributes to the body in the same way; not everyone speaks in tongues or interprets in the corporate setting do they?[8] Here Paul does not discuss the private manifestation of tongues. Questions pertaining to the sphere of usage for private tongues are simply not in view.

This insight is significant for some have suggested that here Paul limits tongues-speech to a few in the community who have been so gifted. D.A. Carson's comments in *Showing the Spirit* are representative of this position.[9] On the basis of the rhetorical question in 1 Cor. 12.30 ('Do all speak in tongues?'), Carson argues that it is inappropriate to insist that all may speak in tongues: not all have the same gift. This principle is central to Carson's dismissal of tongues as evidence of a distinctive post-conversion experience. Yet Carson fails to acknowledge the complexity of the issue. 1 Corinthians 12.30 must be reconciled with 14.5 ('I would like everyone of you to speak in tongues'), a text we shall consider in some detail below.

---

[8] Fee, *First Corinthians*, p. 623.

[9] D.A. Carson, *Showing the Spirit. A Theological Exposition of 1 Corinthians 12-14* (Grand Rapids: Baker, 1987), pp. 42-50.

Furthermore, he does not consider whether the reference in 12.30 is limited to the public manifestation of tongues. If, as the context suggests, this is the case, then the way is open for every believer to be edified personally through the private manifestation of tongues. It is striking that Carson fails to discuss this exegetical option when he acknowledges that, although all are not prophets (12.29), all may prophesy (14.31). Paul's comment in 14.18 ('I thank God that I speak in tongues more than all of you'), coupled with the reference in 14.5 noted above, suggest that Paul considered the private manifestation of tongues to be edifying, desirable, and available to every Christian.[10] It would appear that Carson has misread Paul and inappropriately restricted tongues-speech to a select group within the Christian community.

In short, we should not miss the faulty logic in the case presented by those who, on the one hand, have been quick to cite this text as a clear statement limiting the manifestation of tongues (public or private) to a select group within the church; and yet, on the other hand, have affirmed that everyone can prophesy. If, in spite of the rhetorical question in 12.29 ('Are all prophets?'), it is acknowledged that all can potentially prophesy (usually on the basis of 1 Cor. 14.1, 31), why is it so different with tongues? If, as Turner notes, 'The distinction between the narrower circle of those recognized as 'prophets' and a broader one of those 'able (occasionally) to prophesy' is ... widely accepted', why is it so difficult to see the distinction between tongues exercised 'in the assembly' (the corporate setting) and the exercise of tongues in private, particularly when Paul clearly speaks of these two distinct functions (e.g. public: 1 Cor. 14.27-28; private: 1 Cor. 14.4-5, 18)?[11] It is difficult not to feel that factors other than the text are controlling exegesis at this point. Turner, however, is helpful at this point in that he does offer reasons for his judgment.

Turner argues that there is little in the text which would 'prepare the reader to think Paul's question, 'Not all speak in tongues do

---

[10] Note also 1 Cor. 14.4: 'He who speaks in a tongue edifies himself ...'

[11] The question concerning whether or not there are two distinct gifts of tongues (one for private edification and one for use in the corporate setting) is not germane. What is essential and a point upon which Turner and I agree is that 'Paul distinguishes two spheres of use of tongues – public and private ...' (Turner, 'Experience for All', p. 238).

they?' refers exclusively or primarily to the use of tongues in public worship'.[12] Turner acknowledges that the larger context clearly focuses on problems related to congregational worship (Chapters 8-14), with Chapters 12-14 focusing specifically on the abuse of tongues 'in the assembly'. The immediate context also focuses our attention on the corporate life of the church. Paul, who has just highlighted the importance and uniqueness of each believer's role in the corporate life of the church (note the body metaphor, 1 Cor. 12.12-26), declares in 1 Cor. 12.27, 'Now you are the body of Christ ...' The list of ministries, gifts, and deeds of service and the associated rhetorical questions follow immediately (1 Cor. 12.28-30) and are prefaced with the phrase, 'in the assembly' (1 Cor. 12.28). Elsewhere this phrase very clearly refers to the corporate gathering of believers, the local assembly (1 Cor. 11.18; 14.19, 23, 28, 33, 35). For most this is enough to indicate that Paul has the local congregation at Corinth in view.[13] Fee states the matter clearly: 'Since [v. 28] is coordinate with v. 27, with its emphatic "you are," meaning the church in Corinth, there can be little question that by this phrase ["in the assembly"] Paul also primarily intends the local assembly in Corinth'.[14]

Turner, however, remains unconvinced. In spite of these contextual markers, he argues that Paul here has in mind the church universal rather than the local assembly in Corinth. This judgment follows from Paul's reference to 'apostles' (1 Cor. 12.28, 29). 'There were not regularly (if ever) a plurality of apostles in the Corinthian meetings'.[15] Nevertheless, no doubt feeling the weight of the evidence, Turner largely concedes this point and moves to his major objection.

> Even if Paul has the Corinthian church primarily in mind (cf. 12.27), his description of what God has set 'in the church' cannot easily be restricted in reference to what goes on when 'the church in Corinth' meets in formal assembly for public worship,

---

[12] Turner, 'Experience for All', p. 240.

[13] Fee, *First Corinthians*, p. 618; Dunn, *Jesus and the Spirit*, pp. 262-63; R. Banks, *Paul's Idea of Community* (Grand Rapids: Eerdmans, 1980), pp. 35-37.

[14] Fee, *First Corinthians*, p. 618, n. 13.

[15] Turner, 'Experience for All', p. 240.

as opposed to what happens through believers (individually or as groups) in the variety of contexts that Corinthian life provided.[16]

Turner argues that the rhetorical questions, 'Not all are apostles are they?', 'Not all are prophets are they?', 'Not all work miracles do they?', 'Not all have gifts of healings do they?', indicate that Paul is talking about activities which cannot be restricted to what takes place in the local assembly. Paul is an apostle whether he is shipwrecked at sea, fleeing from persecution, or 'in the church'. Similarly, prophets often prophesy outside the assembly (cf. Acts 21.4, 11) and the working of miracles and gifts of healings are normally described as happening outside the assembly (e.g. Acts 8.36-41; 28.7-8). In the light of all this, Turner asks, how can the reader be expected to discern that when Paul asks, 'Not all speak in tongues do they?', he is asking only about the expression of tongues in the assembly?[17]

Actually, several reasons indicate that this is exactly what we would expect. First, as we have noted, the context clearly focuses our attention on the corporate life of the church. Paul has stressed the need for diversity in the body of Christ. He now illustrates this with concrete examples from the life of the church in Corinth. The list and rhetorical questions of 1 Cor. 12.28-30 offer examples of the variety of ministries and gifts that are exercised in the corporate life of the church. In this context, the references to 'apostles', 'prophets', 'teachers', etc., allude to the diverse *functions* these individuals exercise 'in the assembly'. This is confirmed by the shift in the list from people (apostles, prophets, teachers) to gifts and deeds, literally 'miracles', 'gifts of healing', 'helpful deeds', 'acts of guidance', 'different kinds of tongues'.[18] All of the functions listed here could and quite naturally would have taken place in the local assembly in Corinth and, especially in light of v. 28 ('in the assembly'), Paul's readers most naturally would have viewed the list in this way. The thrust of the rhetorical questions is then abundantly clear: when we gather together, do all function in the same way to build up the body of Christ? Of course not.

---

[16] Turner, 'Experience for All', p. 240.

[17] Turner, 'Experience for All', p. 241.

[18] Fee, *First Corinthians*, pp. 620-22.

Secondly, while Turner correctly notes that some of the ministries noted in these verses (12.28-30) might possibly take place outside of the formal assembly, it must be noted that all of the functions listed here refer to activities that take place in a corporate setting. None of the ministries or actions which Paul lists here can take place in a private setting (that is, by an individual in insolation from others). The only possible exception would be Paul's reference to tongues. However, since elsewhere Paul clearly speaks of a corporate expression of this gift (in contrast to a private expression), Paul's reader would have quite naturally understood the text in this way. That this is indeed what Paul intended is confirmed, not only by the context, but also by the collocation of rhetorical questions pertaining to tongues and the interpretation of tongues (the latter demands a corporate setting; cf. 1 Cor. 14.5) in 1 Cor. 12.30.

Third, Turner's lack of faith in the ability of Paul's readers to pick up on these contextual markers is striking when he himself acknowledges that Paul clearly distinguishes between the private and corporate expressions of the gift of tongues. If Turner can see this distinction in the text, why assume Paul's readers could not? In light of our discussion above, it would be odd if the Corinthians had missed this point. In any event, we need not.

One final point with reference to 1 Cor. 12.28-30 is worth noting. Turner seeks to justify those, like D.A. Carson, who see this passage as restricting tongues to a select few, yet understand prophecy to be available to all. He notes that prophecy is 'an established ministry', and thus some function in the gift more frequently and profoundly than others. While all might prophesy (1 Cor. 14.31), not all are prophets. The problem with tongues, we are told, is that there was no established ministry of tongues, or at least the terminology to speak of such a ministry was lacking and certainly not employed by Paul. Yet is not the distinction between those who exercise the gift of tongues in a corporate setting with interpretation for the edification of all and those who exercise in the gift in a private setting for their own edification rather obvious? Although Paul does not coin a special term for individuals who exercise the gift of tongues in the corporate setting, the distinction between these *functions* is very clear. Indeed, it would appear that the distinction between the corporate exercise of tongues (12.28-30) and the private exercise (14.4-5) is more easily discerned than the distinction between those who prophesy in a particularly profound way and those who do so only occasionally and less powerfully. Does Paul in 12.28-29 refer to the office of the prophet or the function of prophecy more generally? Fee states 'the answer is probably Yes and No'.[19] This ambiguous answer makes my point: the distinction here between the office of prophet and the function of prophecy (Paul actually seems to be stressing the latter) is not as clear as the distinction between the corporate and private expressions of tongues.

What is too often missed in this discussion is that Paul's concern here, whether in relation to prophecy or to tongues, is *not* to delineate who may or may not function in these gifts. Fee correctly notes that Paul's 'rhetoric does not mean, "May all do this?" to which the answer would probably be, "Of course." Rather, it means, "Are all, Do all?" to which the answer is, "Of course not".'[20] In other words, just as Paul in these verses does not intend to exclude anyone from potentially uttering a word of prophecy (all may, but not all do); so also, Paul does not intend to limit anyone from potentially uttering a message in tongues (with interpretation) for the benefit of the church (all may, but not all do). What should be even clearer is that Paul's words here have absolutely nothing to do with limiting the scope of those who manifest tongues in private to a select few.

Paul's Wish (1 Corinthians 14.5)

We now come to the *crux* of the matter. How shall we interpret Paul's words, 'I would like every one of you to speak in tongues, but I would rather have you prophesy' (1 Cor. 14.5a)? This passage has been frequently abused over the years, as Turner correctly notes.[21] Turner, along with Fee, rejects the notion that Paul here, as elsewhere, is 'damning tongues with faint praise'.[22] Turner specifically rejects the notion that in 1 Cor. 14.5a Paul grants 'what he will effectively withdraw through the strategy of the *whole* discourse'.[23]

---

[19] Fee, *First Corinthians*, p. 621.

[20] Fee, *First Corinthians*, p. 623.

[21] See Turner, 'Experience for All', p. 245, and the references he cites in n. 30.

[22] The quote is from Fee, *First Corinthians*, p. 653. For Turner's comments, see Turner, 'Experience for All', p. 245.

[23] Turner, 'Experience for All', p. 245 (italics his).

He acknowledges that Paul values tongues quite highly. As we have seen, Paul explicitly states that the private manifestation of tongues is edifying to the speaker (1 Cor. 14.4) and he himself frequently exercised the gift and was thankful to God for this fact (1 Cor. 14.18). Thus Turner finds little evidence of irony in Paul's wish and regards it as genuine. Yet, and this is the key for Turner, all of this does not mean that Paul felt the wish would actually be realized. It is a genuine wish, but Paul does not expect it to be fulfilled. According to Turner, this judgment is supported by Paul's use of the grammatical construction, 'I would like ... but rather ...', which is also found in 1 Cor. 7.7. Here Paul expresses the wish that all could be celibate as he himself is. 'I wish that all men were as I am. But each man has his own gift from God ...' (1 Cor. 7.7). Turner correctly notes that we would not want to press this 'to mean Paul really does set forth that *everyone can* and (perhaps) *should* be unmarried and celibate'. However, I would add that we know that this wish cannot and should not be universally fulfilled, not because of the grammatical construction Paul uses, but rather because the context explicitly tells us this is the case. As Turner notes, 1 Cor. 7.2-6 tells us of the need that some have for sexual relations in the context of marriage, and the wish is qualified in v. 7 so as to bring out this point. The context of 1 Cor. 14.5 is strikingly different. In 1 Corinthians 14 there is nothing that suggests that here Paul's wish cannot or should not be fulfilled. The context actually suggests the opposite.

1 Corinthians 14.5 forms part of a larger unit (1 Cor. 14.2-5). Paul's argument here can be analyzed in terms of the structure of the passage. The passage contains three couplets that consist of parallel statements concerning tongues and prophecy. Paul has just encouraged the Corinthians 'to eagerly desire spiritual gifts, especially the gift of prophecy' (1 Cor. 14.1). He then tells them why this should be the case ('for', 14.2). Each couplet moves from a description of tongues as beneficial for the individual and thus fitting for the private setting to a description of prophecy as beneficial for the body and thus fitting for the corporate setting. The couplets build to the final point: in the assembly, prophecy is preferred above tongues, unless interpreted, because it is edifying to all.

For

  a) The one who speaks in tongues speaks to God (private setting)
    Indeed, no one understands him
    He speaks mysteries by the Spirit
  b) The one who prophesies speaks to people (corporate setting)
    edification, encouragement, comfort
  a) The one who speaks in tongues edifies himself (private setting)
  b) The one who prophesies edifies the church (corporate setting)
  a) I would like every one of you to speak in tongues (private setting)
  b) but I would rather have you prophesy (corporate setting)

(Thus in the assembly.)

He who prophesies is greater than he who speaks in tongues, unless he interprets, so that the church may be edified.

This analysis of the structure of 1 Cor. 14.2-5 highlights several important aspects of Paul's attitude towards tongues. First, it is evident that for Paul, tongues is edifying and appropriate in its proper context, the private domain. Of course at least some at Corinth did not properly understand this point. Second, Paul's wish that all would speak in tongues (1 Cor. 14.5a), must, as the structure and logic of his argument indicate, refer to the private manifestation of the gift. The contrast with 1 Cor. 14.5b indicates that here Paul is talking about uninterpreted tongues. It would be incomprehensible for Paul to desire that all should speak in tongues without interpretation in the assembly (1 Cor. 14.23). Third, since tongues like prophecy has a positive (albeit largely non-congregational and thus lesser) contribution to make, it would appear that both may be exercised by anyone in the community. As we have noted, nothing in the context suggests Paul's wish that all would speak in tongues cannot or should not be realized. And, the parallelism between 14.5a and 14.5b (and throughout 14.2-4) suggests that both prophecy and tongues are open to all within the community of believers. That is to say, since Paul seems to believe that all may prophesy and indeed encourages the Corinthians to do so (1 Cor. 14.5b; cf. 14.1, 31), it would seem that in light of 1 Cor. 14.5 (cf. 14.18) it is most probable that Paul had a similar attitude toward the private manifestation of tongues. Indeed, if the gift of tongues has merit in its private expression, why would God withhold it?[24]

Of course Paul's primary intent in this passage is not to give his readers a detailed treatment of the private manifestation of tongues. He is, as we have noted, seeking to correct misunderstandings and abuses concerning the exercise of tongues in the assembly. Nevertheless, we may properly ask what implications emerge from Paul's instruction at this point for our question. Although Paul's wish in 1 Cor. 14.5 forms part of a larger argument which seeks to encourage the Corinthians to value prophecy in the assembly, it does offer valuable insight into the mind of the Apostle on this issue. In view of Paul's positive attitude towards the private manifestation of tongues (1 Cor. 14.2-4, 18) and the lack of any clear limitation for the wish beyond placing tongues in the private setting, it is most probable that Paul understood this wish, not only to be genuine, but to express a potentially realizable state of affairs.[25]

Conclusion

Biblical exegesis is the bedrock of sound systematic reflection. Our different and varied systematic formulations reflect our different appraisals of specific texts. In this chapter, I have attempted to explain why I believe Paul encourages us to see the private manifestation of tongues as edifying and available to every believer. Max Turner will probably disagree with my assessment of the biblical data and thus want to formulate matters differently. Nevertheless, there are substantial areas of agreement. By way of conclusion, I

---

[24] Turner notes that Judaism, and especially the OT, anticipated a universal outpouring of prophecy; yet with respect to tongues, the Jewish traditions are virtually silent. So Paul had 'good scriptural grounds' for a universal expectation with respect to prophecy, but not for tongues (Turner, 'An Experience for All', p. 246). However, this misses the important fact that tongues was clearly viewed, at least by Luke, as one expression of prophecy (Acts 2.17-18).

[25] Fee, *First Corinthians*, p. 623. Gerald Hovenden also cautiously sides with me against Turner on this issue (Hovenden, *Speaking in Tongues: The New Testament Evidence in Context* [JPTSup 22; London: Sheffield Academic Press, 2002], pp. 151-59).

would like to highlight several points that I feel are particularly significant.

First, I do believe that Pentecostals are correctly challenging many to reassess their previous rather negative reconstruction of Paul's attitude toward the gift of tongues. 1 Corinthians 12-14 is often treated as Paul's attempt to put down the practice of glossolalia, even though Paul's rhetorical flourishes often contain comments that might at first glance seem to affirm it. This reading of Paul needs to be challenged and, it is noteworthy, that on this point Turner and I are in full agreement.

Secondly, while I believe for the reasons stated above that Paul did believe all could be edified by the private manifestation of tongues, I would agree that the exercise of this gift does not take us to the center of Christian spirituality. There are a wide range of questions theologians must ponder, and while this question is not insignificant, it is not as significant as many. In short, the question of tongues does not take us to the core of the Christian faith and, indeed, does not in my opinion represent the most important theological contribution Pentecostals have to make to the larger body of Christ. I believe that the Pentecostal appraisal of Spirit-baptism has more far-reaching implications for the life of the church.[26]

Thirdly, when Turner questions the appropriateness of seeing in tongues the 'evidence' of Spirit-baptism,[27] he challenges us to recognize the limitations of our human formulations. All theological formulations represent human attempts to come to terms with the significance of the word of God. These human formulations often have strengths and weaknesses. While I believe that the classical Pentecostal doctrine of tongues as the 'initial physical evidence' of baptism in the Holy Spirit captures well the sense of expectation inherent in Paul's words, I would acknowledge that the statement is not without its limitations.[28] The focus on evidence can lead to a

---

[26]See R.P. Menzies, 'Evidential Tongues: An Essay on Theological Method', *Asian Journal of Pentecostal Studies* 1 (1998), pp. 122-23.

[27] Turner, 'Experience for All', pp. 249-50. 'One does not receive the impression that the God of the bible looks particularly favorably on the human search for "proofs" ...'

[28] In academic circles it is common to criticize with condescending tones this doctrinal formulation as stemming from an outdated, modernist perspective (e.g. James K.A. Smith states '"evidence"' is linked to a problematic, modernist, and foundationalist epistemology', *Thinking in Tongues. Pentecostal Contributions to Chris-*

preoccupation with a single, crisis experience. Evidential tongues can also be easily confused with a badge of holiness, an experience that signifies that one has entered into a higher degree of spiritual maturity. At a popular level, Pentecostals have too often succumbed to this Corinthian temptation. Turner's article might serve as a call for Pentecostals to be clearer on these points.

I have found Turner's proddings on the issue of tongues, and particularly Paul's attitude towards the gift, to be extremely helpful. We Pentecostals have at times simply assumed that our position is correct and thus not always thought through carefully nor communicated clearly our various theological positions. We should value friends like Dr. Turner, who through their good-natured proddings challenge us to deal with issues that we might otherwise overlook. This dialogue has challenged me to engage the text in a fresh and rigorous manner and helped me better understand those with whom I disagree. This in turn gives me hope that we may indeed 'follow the way of love' and encourage one another to all move toward the goal of more faithfully reflecting the mind of Christ.

Application

Can those who have not yet spoken in tongues experience Pentecostal power?

This is a question that many of my non-Pentecostal Evangelical friends pose. They feel that Pentecostals view them as 'second class' Christians. Furthermore, they insist that, by definition, any theology that speaks of a baptism in the Spirit that is distinct from conversion must ultimately lead to elitism within the church. I believe that the charge of elitism is only accurate when Pentecostals draw a necessary connection between baptism in the Spirit and Christian maturity or fruit of the Spirit, which they generally do not.[29] As we have noted, Pentecostals normally describe baptism in the Spirit as an empowering for mission. Ideally, Christian maturity and missio-

---

tian Philosophy [Grand Rapids: Eerdmans, 2010], p. 124, n. 1). Yet this critique misses the fact that, as we have seen, Luke himself highlights the evidential or sign value of tongues. This suggests that the issue addressed here cannot be so easily dismissed as merely reflecting the concerns of one specific, historically defined group.

[29] For more on this topic see Chapter 15, 'The Baptism in the Spirit and the Fruit of the Spirit', in Menzies, *Spirit and Power*, pp. 201-208.

logical power go hand in hand, but in practice we see that this is not always the case. The church at Corinth was gifted – we might say that they had charismatic power – but they were far from mature.[30] 'As we walk forward in the ways of the Spirit, we will likely encounter moments of refreshment that are ethically transforming and missiologically inspiring. But one dimension may develop without the other.'[31] Thus, Pentecostals should be quick to acknowledge that speaking in tongues is not a sign of Christian maturity. Baptism in the Spirit (in the Lukan sense) and speaking in tongues are no guarantee of a life dramatically marked by the fruit of the Spirit.

Yet, we still must address our central question. What about missiological power? Can those who have not yet spoken in tongues experience Pentecostal power? We must be very careful here not to limit God. Since we are describing experiential realities, and God delights to empower his people, it would not be wise to offer a legalistic response. In short, I do believe that many Christians who would not consider themselves to be Pentecostal and who have not spoken in tongues do experience, in varying degrees, Pentecostal power. We might call them 'anonymous Pentecostals'. Who can fathom the depths of the human psyche or the mind of God? Who can explain why some find it difficult to burst forth in tongues and others do not? For whatever reason, whether due to long-standing theological prejudices or one's psychological makeup, some earnest Christians find it difficult to experience this gift. I am convinced that many of these Christians do experience Pentecostal power, even though they might not recognize it as such.

Here, however, I believe that it is important to qualify our response in two important ways. First, while it may be possible to experience in varying degrees Pentecostal power without speaking in tongues, it should be noted that this is not the full biblical experience. This is not Luke's Spirit-inspired intention for us. The full apostolic experience as described in Acts includes the experience of tongues. Additionally, although 'anonymous Pentecostals' may experience Pentecostal power, I am also convinced that they would experience this power more frequently and to a greater extent if they consciously embraced the Pentecostal perspective. You see,

---

[30] Compare 1 Cor. 1.5-7 with 1 Cor. 3.1-4.
[31] Menzies, *Spirit and Power*, p. 207.

Pentecostal experience is encouraged and directed by the biblical models in Acts and it is reinforced by the symbolic message of tongues. In short, there is power in the narrative and in this expressive gift (i.e. tongues). Together, they facilitate and guide our appropriation of Pentecostal power.

Let's pose the question another way. Can you be baptized in the Spirit without speaking in tongues? Perhaps. But why would we want to settle for anything less than the full apostolic experience? Why refuse what Paul describes as an edifying and encouraging gift?

Good
Q

Of course the pastoral issues here are real and must be addressed. What do we say to earnest Christians who have sought the Pentecostal baptism for an extended period of time (perhaps years) and still have not spoken in tongues? I would say the following: Do not allow your inability to speak in tongues to discourage you in your pursuit of God or his mission. Your lack of tongues is not a sign of immaturity nor of God's displeasure. I do not know why you find it difficult to experience this gift. But I do know that speaking in tongues is only one way among many that God encourages and edifies his children. Keep moving forward in your walk with Jesus. Stay hungry for his presence and allow him to lead you. Follow the models in Acts. Remain open and you may yet find that he surprises you. Be encouraged by the gifts expressed within the community of faith. Rejoice with others when they speak in tongues and allow their utterances to serve as reminders of our common bond with the apostolic church. Remember that speaking in tongues is not a sign of Christian maturity nor is a lack of tongues a sign of immaturity. Above all, know that God delights to use you – and he will – for his glory.

Reflection Questions

1. Some feel that Paul's rhetorical question in 1 Cor. 12.30, 'Do all speak in tongues?' clearly indicates that the gift of tongues is limited to a select few. Why does Menzies disagree with this position? What do you think?

2. Why is the context, which focuses on the corporate setting, so crucial for our understanding of Paul's intent in 1 Cor. 12.30?

3. Turner argues that while Paul's wish in 1 Cor. 14.5, 'I would like every one of you to speak in tongues', was genuine, it was a wish Paul knew could not be realized. What support does Turner offer for this position? How does Menzies counter?

4. What does the structure of 1 Cor. 14.2-5 tell us about Paul's perspective?

5. What is Paul's primary intent in 1 Corinthians 14? What are the implications that emerge from Paul's words of instruction for our question concerning the availability of tongues? Does this impact your attitude toward speaking in tongues? Does it change the way that you pray?

6

RECONCILING LUKE AND PAUL:
TONGUES AS A SIGN

Not long ago while I was writing a book on Pentecostal identity and
the way in which it's core elements are rooted in Luke's narrative, I
began to consider a question. It is a question of significance for
Pentecostals, but it is one that, to my knowledge, has not been seriously addressed. Shortly after I completed my writing project, yet
while this question was still fresh in my mind, I received a note
from an Assemblies of God pastor. He raised, in a slightly different
form, the question that I had been pondering. How do we reconcile
Luke's positive emphasis on speaking in tongues as a sign that
serves to strengthen and encourage the Christian community and
that may, in special instances, have apologetic value as well (Acts
2.1-22, 33; 10.44-46; 19.1-7; cf. Lk. 11.9-13) with Paul's apparently
disparaging comments about tongues as a 'negative' sign in 1 Cor.
14.20-25? Of course, our answer to this question carries with it very
practical and important implications. How we answer this question,
as my pastoral colleague perceived, will impact our understanding
of 'order' in church services. It will dictate, to a large extent, the
contexts in which we might encourage people to seek to be baptized in the Holy Spirit (Acts 1.8; 2.4), since the biblical model for
this experience includes glossolalia. Indeed, if we accept a literal
reading of Paul over against Luke at this point, then we would not
allow any expression of tongues in our church services unless they

were interpreted.[1] Of course, this is precisely what many non-Pentecostal (and perhaps not a few Pentecostal) churches do.

However, the question must be asked, is this really fair to Luke? Does it do justice to the full canon of Scripture? And cannot Luke and Paul be reconciled in a manner that actually does justice to the intention of both inspired authors? These are the questions that this chapter shall seek to address.

Tongues as a Sign – Luke's Perspective

We have already spent more than a few pages delineating the striking and conspicuous role that speaking in tongues plays in Luke's two-volume work. We may summarize our discussion by noting that Luke presents us with a formidable resume for speaking in tongues. Luke expected that tongues would continue to play a positive role in his church and ours, both of which are located in 'these last days'. In Luke's view, every believer can manifest this spiritual gift. So, Luke encourages every believer to pray for prophetic anointings (Lk. 11.13), experiences of Spirit-inspired exultation from which power and praise flow; experiences similar to those modeled by Jesus (Lk. 3.21-22; 10.21) and the early church (Acts 2.4; 10.46; 19.6). Luke believed that these experiences would typically include glossolalia, which he considered a special form of prophetic speech. More specifically, Luke presents speaking in tongues as a powerful and edifying sign – a sign that reminds us of our calling as end-time prophets and that testifies to the majesty and exalted status of Jesus.

It is worth noting that Luke presents tongues as a positive sign both for believers (e.g. Acts 10.46-47) and unbelievers (e.g. Acts 2.5-13, 33, 37) alike.[2] Speaking in tongues, as a special form of prophecy, marks the disciples of Jesus as the true heirs of Joel's prophecy and validates their message.

---

[1] Presumably, this would exclude expressions of glossolalia in corporate praise and prayer, such as 'singing in tongues'.
[2] So also Mk 16.17.

Tongues as a Sign – Paul's Perspective

This analysis of Luke's perspective calls us to reconsider Paul's attitude towards speaking in tongues, and particularly his perspective on tongues as a sign. A careful reading of 1 Corinthians 12-14 reveals that while Paul holds the private manifestation of tongues in high regard,[3] his purpose here is clearly polemical. He seeks to correct the Corinthian abuse of the gift of tongues. In the pages that follow I shall attempt to shed light on the problem that Paul addresses, the specific nature of his response, and more specifically, how we should understand his words in 1 Cor. 14.20-25. Finally, I will draw out the implications of Paul's instructions for our understanding of church order and practice today and seek to integrate these findings with Luke's contributions.

The Problem at Corinth

At least some of the Corinthians appear to have viewed tongues as an expression of a superior level of spirituality. Thus, they valued tongues above other gifts and, in the context of corporate meetings, their spiritual elitism often found expression in unintelligible outbursts that disrupted meetings and did not build up the church.[4] This basic reconstruction of the problem at Corinth has found widespread acceptance. However, one matter is less clear. Were all of the Corinthians caught up in this elitist form of spirituality (and thus standing in opposition to Paul) or was the church itself divided over the issue? We noted in the previous chapter that the former position has been advocated by Gordon Fee and the latter by Christopher Forbes.[5]

Max Turner, following closely the lead of Forbes, suggests that at Corinth the gift of tongues was exercised by some to establish or reinforce their position as a member of the spiritual elite. The exercise of tongues was, then, a part of the 'power games' that divided the church at Corinth.[6] This being the case, we can see that Paul seeks to correct the Corinthians' misunderstanding: he highlights

---

[3] So also Fee, *First Corinthians*, p. 659.

[4] Turner, 'Experience for All', pp. 235-36.

[5] Fee, *First Corinthians*, pp. 4-15; Forbes, *Prophecy*, pp. 14-16, 171-75, 182-87, 260-64.

[6] Turner, 'Experience for All', p. 237.

the variety and origin of God's gracious gifts (1 Corinthians 12, esp. vv. 4-6), that everyone has a role to play (1 Cor. 12.11-27), and that edification is the key goal (1 Cor. 12.7). Specifically, with reference to tongues, he insists that in the assembly, unless tongues are interpreted, they do not edify the church and thus prophecy is to be preferred (1 Cor. 14.2-5). In the context of his argument that prophecy is greater than tongues in the assembly, Paul also states that the private manifestation of tongues is edifying to the speaker and, furthermore, that it is not limited to an elite group, but rather available to all (1 Cor. 14.5, 18). In other words, just as Paul notes that he is no stranger to tongues and thus qualified to speak of the gift's significance, so also Paul seeks to undermine the Corinthians' improper sense of superiority with his comments concerning the universality of the gift.

Fee, conversely, suggests that we should see the entire church standing in opposition to Paul. The church as a whole was caught up in these elitist ideas and felt that their exercise of tongues displayed their superior wisdom and spirituality in relation to Paul.[7] Regardless of the specific makeup of the elitist faction, all are agreed that the key problem at Corinth with reference to tongues was the abuse of the gift 'in the assembly' (that is, when the church gathered together; cf. 1 Cor. 12.28; 14.4-6, 9-19). We can envision the elitist group reveling in their *public display* of tongues, even though there likely were others who exercised the gift in private such as Paul (1 Cor. 14.18).[8] The elitists viewed this public display of 'speaking mysteries' (14.2) as a sign of their special knowledge and position, and superior to any private usage. Of course, with this flawed thinking, Paul cannot agree.

Paul's Response to the Problem

So, Paul seeks to correct the immature thinking, attitudes, and actions of the elitist group at Corinth. In addition to challenging the basis for these elitist views as noted above, Paul specifically challenges the Corinthian's exercise of tongues at two key points. First,

---

[7] Fee, *First Corinthians*, pp. 4-15.

[8] As stated above, the contrast between 1 Cor. 14.18 ('I thank God I speak in tongues more than you all') and 14.19 ('But, in the church …') indicates that Paul's autobiographical comments in 14.18 refer to the private exercise of tongues.

he admonishes the church at Corinth to limit the public expression of tongues in a given meeting to two or three speakers, and these messages in tongues must be interpreted (1 Cor. 14.28). 'If there is no interpreter', Paul declares, 'the speaker should keep quiet' (1 Cor. 14.28). Second, Paul counters the Corinthian understanding of tongues as a sign. Here we must grapple with a passage of critical importance for our present study: 1 Cor. 14.20-25.

The structure of 1 Cor. 14.20-25 is rather straightforward, although its meaning is much more difficult to ascertain. The structure may be outlined as follows:

1. Exhortation (v. 20). 'Brothers, stop thinking like children ...'
2. Argument (vv. 21-25)
   a. Quotation (v. 21). "Through men of strange tongues ... I will speak to this people, but even then they will not listen to me', says the Lord'.
   b. Assertion 1 (v. 22a). 'Tongues, then, are a sign, not for believers, but for unbelievers'.
      Assertion 2 (v. 22b). 'Prophecy, however, is for believers, not for unbelievers'.
   c. Illustration 1 (v. 23). 'So if ... everyone speaks in tongues ... will they not say that you are out of your mind?'
      Illustration 2 (v. 24). 'But if ... while everybody is prophesying ... he will fall down and worship God, exclaiming, 'God is really among you!"

This passage is widely acknowledged to be one of the most difficult to fathom in all of Paul's writing.[9] The key problem centers in v. 22, and involves its relationship to the OT quotation that precedes (v. 21) and to the illustrations that follow (vv. 23-25). The illustrations of vv. 23-25 appear to contradict the assertions of v. 22. How can tongues be a sign for unbelievers, when they cause the unbelievers to declare that the Christians who utter them are 'out of [their] minds?' And how can prophecy not be a sign for unbelievers, when it results in them declaring, 'God is really among you!'

---

[9] S.J. Kistemaker notes that 'this text has been problematic for every interpreter' (Kistemaker, *1 Corinthians* [Grand Rapids: Baker, 1993], p. 500).

Pondering these and related problems have caused more than one pastor to lose considerable sleep, and for good reason. Chrysostom stated it well, 'The difficulty at this place is great, which seems to arise from what is said'.[10] In spite of the considerable challenges posed by this text, most scholars agree that Paul's position is most clearly seen in the illustrations of vv. 23-25. The critical appraisal of tongues as an evangelistic tool and the positive assessment of the impact of prophecy contained in this these verses seem to square well with the general tenor of Paul's argument in 1 Corinthians 12-14. How all of this relates to the OT quotation (v. 21) and the assertions of v. 22 is another matter.

Two answers to this vexing question appear to commend themselves. One response, that offered by Fee and a host of others, suggests that the problem lies in how we understand the word 'sign'.[11] The OT quotation, we are told, indicates that the term 'sign' carries with it a negative sense: it is a negative sign, one that signals a hardness of heart and God's judgment. Thus, tongues, which are not understood by the unbelievers, serve as a sign, albeit a negative one, for them – a sign of judgment. Prophecy, on the other hand, is presented as a positive sign, one that leads to belief. Although this is undoubtedly one of the better solutions offered for this riddle, it is not without its flaws. It does require that we understand the term 'sign' to function in different ways when applied to tongues and prophecy respectively, even though these terms appear in the same sentence.

A better solution, I believe, has been advanced by Bruce Johanson.[12] Johanson argues that in this passage Paul utilizes a rhetorical device known well among the ancient Greeks, the diatribe. Thus, after offering a rather loose paraphrase of Isa. 28.11-12,[13] Paul has an imaginary opponent voice his opposing view in the form of a rhetorical question. The rhetorical question is actually an inference

[10] Chrysostom, *1 Cor. Hom.*, 36.2 (as cited in Anthony Thiselton, *The First Epistle to the Corinthians* [Grand Rapids: Eerdmans, 2000], p. 1122).

[11] Fee, *First Corinthians*, pp. 676-88; Craig S. Keener, *1-2 Corinthians* (New Cambridge Bible Commentary; Cambridge: Cambridge University Press, 2005), pp. 114-15.

[12] Bruce C. Johanson, 'Tongues, a Sign for Unbelievers?', *NTS* 25 (1979), pp. 180-203.

[13] Johanson, 'Tongues, a Sign for Unbelievers?', pp. 182, 193.

drawn from the preceding quote from Isaiah: 'Are tongues, then, meant as a sign not for believers but for unbelievers?' (v. 22a).[14] It should be noted that in Johanson's view, this is not Paul's perspective. It is rather the perspective of Paul's opponents. In the opponents' minds, the question should be answered with a resounding 'yes'. So, according to Johanson, the key phrases in 1 Cor. 14.22 ('tongues … are a sign … for unbelievers' and 'prophecy … for believers') give voice to the view of Paul's opponents rather than that of Paul himself.

This reading offers a coherent explanation of the relationship between the paraphrase from Isa. 28.11-12 and the opponents' inference (v. 22). Johanson notes that Paul's paraphrase, which deviates from both the MT and the LXX, omits the intelligible message (Isa. 28.12) spoken by the 'Lord' (MT) or 'they' (LXX) to which 'this people' refuse to listen. Thus, in Paul's version, the hearers refuse to listen to the *unintelligible* speech of the 'foreigners'. This suggests that the quotation either stems from the Corinthian glossolalists or was tailored by Paul to reflect their views. Whichever approach is taken (Johanson opts for the latter view),[15] the essential meaning of the quotation from Isa. 28.11-12 remains the same: the 'people' of v. 21 refers to believers and the point of the quotation (as understood by Paul's opponents) is to say that tongues, although ineffective for instructing Christians, serve as an authenticating, apologetic sign for unbelievers.

After this reference to tongues as a sign for unbelievers ('Are tongues, then, meant as a sign not for believers but for unbelievers

---

[14] Changing punctuation is not a problem since the earliest manuscripts contain hardly any punctuation. The question mark, in particular, was not used until the ninth century. See Bruce Metzger, *The Text of the New Testament* (New York: Oxford, 1964), p. 27. On the grammatical feasibility of this proposal, see Johanson, 'Tongues, a Sign for Unbelievers?', pp. 189, 193. David Garland argues that Johanson's view 'fails to take into account the οὖν (*oun*) in 14.23', which he sees as pointing to the consequences of v. 22 (*1 Corinthians* [Grand Rapids: Baker, Academic, 2003], p. 649). However, as Dr. George Flattery points out, οὖν can be used with an adversative sense ('but' or 'however') or, I would add, even to express certainty ('certainly' or 'to be sure'; cf. 1 Cor. 3.5), both of which would fit with Johanson's view. See W. Bauer *et al.*, *A Greek-English Lexicon of the New Testament and Other Early Christian Literature* (Chicago: University of Chicago Press, 2nd edn, 1979), p. 593, and George M. Flattery, *Spiritual Persons, Gifts, and Churches: A Commentary on 1 Corinthians 12-14* (Springfield, MO: Network211, 2015), pp. 173-89 for his helpful comments.

[15] Johanson, 'Tongues, a Sign for Unbelievers?', p. 193.

...'), Paul then has his imaginary opponent blunder on by saying, '... while prophecy is meant as a sign not for unbelievers but for believers?' (v. 22b). It may well be that there were two factions at Corinth, both of which were vying for authority and power in the church: one emphasized the gift of prophecy; the other, the gift of tongues. Indeed, Johanson asserts that 'the evidence ... points strongly in the direction that there was in particular a confrontation between prophets and glossolalists in Corinth'.[16] He points out that while Paul seems to strengthen the hand of the prophets, he is not totally uncritical of their behavior as well. Paul censures both groups (e.g. 1 Cor. 13.2, 8-9; 14.28-33a, 37-40).

Johanson's reading of 1 Cor. 14.20-25, particularly his thesis that v. 22 gives voice to the Corinthian glossolalists' view, finds support in one other previously overlooked piece of historical evidence. It should be noted that in the New Testament the term 'sign' (σημεῖον) is utilized in conjunction with speaking in tongues in three texts: Mk 16.17 ('these signs will accompany those who believe ... they will speak in new tongues'); Acts 2.19; and 1 Cor. 14.22. We have already noted that the points of connection between Mk 16.9-20 and Luke's narrative are particularly striking. These texts from Luke–Acts and 'the long ending' of Mark clearly bear witness to early, underlying tradition.[17] They also indicate that this early tradition included the idea that tongues serve as a positive, authenticating sign within the Christian community.[18] It seems evident that this tradition was known by and influenced Christians in the church at Corinth. Paul's instruction in 1 Corinthians 12-14 indicates that at least some of these Christians had taken this idea (i.e. that tongues serves as a positive sign), rooted in the tradition, and applied it in extreme and destructive ways for self-centered reasons. Nevertheless, 1 Cor. 14.22 also bears witness to the existence and relatively wide dissemination of this tradition in the early church. Of

---

[16] Johanson, 'Tongues, a Sign for Unbelievers?', p. 196.

[17] Whether or not one accepts 'the long ending' of Mark as the inspired word of God, the historical value of Mk 16.9-20 cannot be questioned. This text was composed at the very latest in the early second century and bears witness to the faith and practice of the early church.

[18] Contra James A. Kelhoffer, who notes the connections between Mk 16.9-20 and Luke–Acts, but claims that only Mark presents tongues as an ongoing sign for believers beyond the apostles (*Miracle*, pp. 141-47, 281).

course, the existence of this tradition makes Johanson's thesis all the more plausible.

However we read 1 Cor. 14.20-25, it appears that there was a group at Corinth that viewed tongues as a positive sign (this is clearly the case if Johanson is correct). In spite of the immature, selfish, and divisive nature of their outlook, this group did see tongues as a positive and encouraging sign of their community's (perhaps too narrowly defined) connection to the calling and power of the apostolic church. Additionally, as our analysis of 1 Cor. 14.20-25 reveals, they also felt that tongues served an evangelistic purpose. They viewed glossolalia as an authenticating sign and, as such, a sign with apologetic value. Of course, given what we read in Acts 2 and also Mk 16.17, we can understand how this view developed in the early church. In fact, it would appear that there were others, in addition to this faction at Corinth, that held to similar views – that is, others who viewed tongues as a positive and significant sign, both for believers in the community (it was a mark of their identity as end-time prophets and a testimony to Jesus' exalted status) and, in some instances, for non-believers outside the community (as at Pentecost, tongues might validate the proclamation of the gospel). Many in the communities represented by the Gospel of Luke and the Gospel of Mark must have held to similar views.

This brings us back to our central question. How do we reconcile these differing views? How do we understand Paul's polemical thrust, where he challenges this positive appraisal of tongues as a sign, when at the same time we see evidence for it in the book of Acts (and the Gospel of Mark). I believe the answer to this problem is to be found in a careful analysis of Paul's argument and, in particular, his underlying motives. To this analysis we now turn.

Tongues as a Sign – Paul's Concerns

Our analysis of Paul's argument above highlights with clarity one important fact. Paul was addressing a specific problem at Corinth. This is an important observation, one that should impact how we understand and apply Paul's instructions to the church at Corinth. Because Paul is addressing a specific problem, we should be cautious about making sweeping judgments concerning normative rules for church order. This is particularly the case when we cannot define with certainty the exact nature of the problem.

A good, cautionary example for us is found in 1 Cor. 14.34: '...
women should remain silent in the churches'. Is this a principle that
should guide the practice of every church? Or, as I believe to be the
case, is Paul here addressing a problem specific to the church at
Corinth?[19] In other words, would Paul have laid down this guideline
in every church he encountered or were there elements unique to
the congregation at Corinth that called for this very special, specific
rule? As we assess Paul's guidelines for the use of tongues in corporate gatherings at Corinth, we should consider carefully whether
here too we need to distinguish between transcendent, universally
applicable principles and rules that are contextually specific. This is
particularly the case given the fact that Paul clearly sees value in the
private manifestation of tongues and other passages in the New
Testament, most notably those in the book of Acts, bear witness to
a fuller, more complex view. All of this calls us to take another look
at Paul's perspective, particularly his motives.

A review of Paul's argument reveals that he has two overriding
concerns with the manner in which tongues were being exercised in
the church gatherings at Corinth. First, Paul was clearly upset with
the lack of concern for intelligibility in church. This concern comes
to the forefront time and time again in 1 Corinthians 14. After noting that the one who speaks in tongues 'utters mysteries' (1 Cor.
14.2) and does not edify others (1 Cor. 14.4), Paul declares, 'he who
prophesies is greater than one who speaks in tongues, unless he interprets' (1 Cor. 14.5).[20] Paul queries, 'unless you speak intelligible
words with your tongue, how will anyone know what you are saying?' (1 Cor. 14.9). And finally, he admonishes them to 'stop thinking like children' (1 Cor. 14.20). Tongues should not, Paul declares,
take the place of proclamation or instruction – the intelligible messages found in prophetic utterances (1 Cor. 14.23-25). Indeed, Paul
concludes by laying down the law: 'If anyone speaks in a tongue ...
someone must interpret' (1 Cor. 14.27).

On this reading of the evidence, it would appear that Paul's concern is not specifically with tongues or even the expression of
tongues in the corporate setting. His concern is with the abuse of

---

[19] For a discussion of the hermeneutical issues, see Paul Elbert, *Pastoral Letter
to Theo: An Introduction to Interpretation and Women's Ministries* (Eugene, OR: Wipf &
Stock, 2008).

[20] This translation follows the NIV (1984 edition).

tongues, or more precisely, the overuse of tongues in the corporate setting. It is apparent, as we read Paul's directives, that at Corinth tongues were taking the place of intelligible messages, whether for the edification of believers or for the purpose of evangelizing non-believers. Notice how in the illustration in 1 Cor. 14.23 Paul refers to 'everyone' speaking in tongues with the result being that others do not understand. The implication is that tongues were taking the place of or totally eclipsing intelligible proclamation. The abuse was so great that Paul felt that strict guidelines had to be put in place.

When we recognize that in 1 Corinthians 12-14 Paul is dealing with a problem specific to the church at Corinth and that Paul's primary concern has to do with the manner in which tongues were eclipsing intelligible utterances, then we read his guidelines on church order with fresh eyes. We wisely become more cautious concerning an overly rigid application of these guidelines in our contemporary settings. We consider the situation in our church services and ask, 'Are our meetings dominated by unintelligible utterances in tongues? Is there little time for intelligible proclamation of the gospel or instruction in the ways of God?' I think the answer to this question is sadly all too evident for the vast majority of our churches. Unbridled enthusiasm is probably not the primary problem with which we must grapple. In other words, we have little to fear when it comes to this concern of Paul.

However, I would note that Paul's polemic clearly issues from a second and perhaps more significant concern. Paul was disturbed by the fact that a group in the church at Corinth was speaking in tongues as a means of establishing their superior status in relation to other believers. In this way, they were also vying for power and authority in the church. Paul seeks to correct this immature, childish, and destructive behavior. He does so by highlighting the rich variety and origin of God's gracious gifts (1 Corinthians 12, esp. vv. 4-6). He emphasizes that in the assembly everyone has a role to play (1 Cor. 12.11-27) and that edification is the key goal (1 Cor. 12.7). Ultimately, he declares, 'If I speak in tongues ... but have not love, I am only a resounding gong or a clanging cymbal' (1 Cor. 13.1). Yet, once again, we must be careful to identify Paul's real concern. Here, I would suggest, it is imperative that we distinguish between Paul's disapproval of twisted motives and the actions produced by these improper motives. In other words, Paul's imperatives con-

cerning church order appear to be largely influenced by the twisted
motives that governed at least one faction's exercise of tongues. It is
debatable, given a different setting with a more mature group of
Christians, whether Paul would lay down similar guidelines.

In short, I would suggest that Paul's attitude towards tongues as
a sign might not be so different from that of Luke after all. Once
we recognize the polemical nature of Paul's words in 1 Corinthians
12-14 and the underlying concerns that shape his argument and related imperatives, we find that Paul may be more appreciative of the
sign-value of tongues than is often recognized. Paul clearly recognizes the edifying nature of glossolalia for the individual. Would this
not include the fact that tongues call us to recognize our connection
with the apostolic church?[21] Would not Paul affirm that tongues
serve to remind us that we are end-time prophets empowered to
bear witness for Jesus?[22] Would he not agree that Spirit-inspired
language, which finds its ultimate source in the Spirit-baptizer, testifies to Jesus' true identity?[23] Since Paul refers with approval to 'singing in tongues' and appears open to various forms of Spirit-inspired
prayer and praise,[24] I think it is evident that Paul would recognize
the value of uninterpreted tongues in corporate worship as long as
it is expressed communally, such as in concert prayer or praise, and
not as the focal point of an isolated event. In other words, if our
expression of tongues in the context of corporate worship does not
disrupt or eclipse intelligible forms of address, such as proclamation, instruction, or prophecy, then I find it hard to believe that
Paul would object. Paul might even affirm the value of tongues in
an evangelistic setting, if they are expressed in conjunction with intelligible proclamation and not disruptive of it. After all, it was Paul
who declared, 'my message and my preaching were not with wise
and persuasive words, but with a demonstration of the Spirit's power' (1 Cor. 2.4). As in so many matters, for Paul the underlying mo-
tive was crucial. If tongues are expressed in love and not out of self-
seeking motives, then their potential value increases exponentially.

---

[21] See 1 Cor. 2.2-5; 1 Thess. 5.19.

[22] See 1 Cor. 1.2, 4-9; 2 Tim. 1.6-8.

[23] See 1 Cor. 12.3, which has points of similarity with Lk. 11.13; Rom. 8.23,
26; 2 Cor. 5.1-4.

[24] See 1 Cor. 14.15; Eph. 5.19; 6.18; and Col. 3.16.

Conclusion: Reconciling Luke and Paul

I have suggested that Luke and Paul's respective attitudes towards tongues, particularly tongues as an edifying or positive sign, are not so different after all. In fact, when Paul's argument in 1 Corinthians 12-14 is understood against the backdrop of the situation at Corinth and his primary concerns, Paul's references to speaking in tongues take on fresh meaning. Indeed, when the specific rules that Paul lays down for order in worship are evaluated in the light of this larger context and his concerns, a rigid application of these imperatives in our contemporary settings appears to be quite misguided. I would like to summarize the implications of our study for the life of the church in catechetical fashion — that is, with a series of questions and answers.

Question 1. Can tongues serve as an evangelistic tool?

Yes, but this appears to be very rare. The account of the Pentecostal outpouring of the Spirit in Acts 2 is the only biblical record of this taking place. And it should be noted that here speaking in tongues takes the special form of xenolalia. Thus, 'Jews from every nation under heaven' (Acts 2.5) understood the tongues of Acts 2. Nevertheless, numerous instances of similar phenomenon in more recent times have been recorded by credible scholars.[25] It is certainly possible that God may choose to work in this manner today. It is also possible that unintelligible tongues (glossolalia) might be used in conjunction with proclamation to arrest the hearer's attention and authenticate the message. However, there is also the very real danger that, as Paul's words in 1 Cor. 14.23-25 attest, tongues may be exercised in a disruptive and inappropriate way. Indeed, they may hinder evangelism. Thus, Paul forbids this evangelistic use of tongues as the normal practice in the assembly. I would suggest that only in very special cases, certainly not as the normal practice of the church, and only in conjunction with intelligible witness should tongues be exercised with an evangelistic purpose in view.

---

[25] See Jordan May, *Global Witness to Pentecost: The Testimony of 'Other Tongues'* (Cleveland, TN: Cherohala Press, 2013).

Question 2. Should tongues be banned from our church services unless they are interpreted?

No, I believe that an overly rigid application of Paul's imperatives in 1 Cor. 14.27-28 misunderstands Paul's underlying concern and purpose. Paul appears to be quite open to various forms of Spirit-inspired prayer and praise (Eph. 5.19; 6.18). Additionally, Luke's record in Acts suggests that tongues were edifying and encouraging in various corporate contexts. With this mind, I believe that both Paul and Luke call us to recognize the value of uninterpreted tongues in corporate worship as long as they are expressed communally, such as in concert prayer or praise, and not disruptive of proclamation, instruction, or prophecy.

Question 3. Is it appropriate during our corporate gatherings (generally, but not necessarily, at the conclusion) to call people to collectively seek God's empowering, complete with manifestations of tongues?

By all means, Yes! Our churches desperately need to establish times when we come together for the purpose of prayer and to collectively seek all that God has for us. This will inevitably lead to experiences of spiritual rapture, those moments when various individuals are baptized in the Holy Spirit and burst forth in glossolalic praise (Acts 2.4). This was the practice and experience of those early Pentecostal pioneers as well as the early church (Acts 1.14; 2.1-4).

Luke, in particular, emphasizes that in these moments, tongues serve as a powerful sign, both to the individual and to the community. It is a sign that reminds us of our calling as end-time prophets and that testifies to the majesty and exalted status of Jesus. I am confident that with this Paul would agree.

Application

On one occasion I arranged for a team to minister in a Miao (a minority group in China) village that I had visited in the past. The team was made up of 12 people. Because of our numbers, I arranged for a van to take us as far up the mountain as possible. The village we were to visit was located high in the mountains in a remote and very poor area of our province. The road conditions were rough and finally, with a gasp, the driver pulled over and said that he had driven as far as possible. We would need to hike the rest of the way.

After a short hike, we arrived to the sort of welcome that only the Miao can give. Believers lined the path singing songs of welcome and encouragement. They led us in this manner into the church. Although the population of the village is less than 200, a sea of over 250 smiling faces had packed into the church. This village and its church are the center of Christian activity in the area and many come from surrounding villages to worship there.

The service began and I was quickly reminded that there are few things so humbling as participating in a Miao worship service. You see, the Miao assume that everyone can sing. They are wonderful singers and their choirs are renowned for the exquisite beauty of their songs. It does no good to protest – visitors must always contribute at least one song. I had prepared the group in advance, so we marched up to the front of the church and sang our Chinese renditions of a few simple choruses. Afterwards, the Miao choir assembled at the front and began to sing. The power and beauty of their worship was breathtaking. Our team sat in awe as these simple people from the mountains – a people who, prior to receiving the gospel a little over one hundred years ago, were viewed as savages – sang songs that would have been welcomed in any cathedral in the world. And then their children's choir sang. It was wonderful.

When the singing came to an end our team began to share about God's love and his power to change lives. After a couple of testimonies, my friend spoke from Acts 2 about the Pentecostal experience. He shared how God had been pouring out his Spirit on many – men, women and children – in their church and encouraged the Miao believers to open their hearts to God's gifts. In spite of the simplicity of my translation, the message struck a chord in the hearts of the Miao. After the message, we asked for those who wanted prayer to stand. The entire congregation rose to their feet. Our team fanned out among the people and we all began to lay hands on the people and pray. The Spirit filled the place and many began to cry, speak in tongues, shake and worship with a loud voice. It was Pentecost all over again, but this time in the mountains of China. I had never seen anything like this in a Miao church. The Miao tend to be rather formal and reserved in manner and worship. But here, an incredible sense of hunger for and openness to the things of the Spirit permeated the place. Formalities were laid aside as people entered into the presence of God.

In the midst of all this I noticed that the driver of our van was standing in the congregation and, with wide eyes, taking it all in. I walked over and asked him what he thought about all that was going on. He replied, 'This is wonderful. I am deeply moved'. I asked him if he knew Jesus. He replied, 'No, not yet; but I am ready!' The power of God's presence and the authentic nature of the worship that he witnessed had clearly impacted him. I shared the gospel with this man and then led him in the sinner's prayer. His face radiated with joy as we returned home that day.

Is it time to reassess our priorities and perceptions regarding dramatic displays of God's presence in our worship services? Does your church make room for the expression of gifts of the Spirit in the corporate setting? Do we make time collectively to seek the face of God in prayer and bask in his presence?

Reflection Questions

1. Menzies notes that Luke views tongues as a positive sign, while Paul seems to have a different perspective. How does he reconcile these two seemingly different perspectives?

2. 1 Corinthians 14.20-25 is a notoriously difficult text to understand. According to the author, the key to understanding this passage is found in recognizing that the words in v. 22 represent the position of Paul's opponents rather than that of Paul himself. Does this make sense to you?

3. The author argues that we must understand Paul's real concerns here if we are to apply his words in our contemporary situation in an appropriate way. He insists that when we approach 1 Corinthians 12-14 with a sensitivity to the polemical nature of Paul's argument, we find that Paul is more appreciative of the sign-value of tongues than is often recognized. Do you agree?

4. How might a fresh appreciation for Paul's real concerns and intent in 1 Corinthians 12-14 impact our attitude towards the expression of tongues in our church meetings?

5. Do you feel that we should make room for singing in the Spirit during corporate worship? Do you sense a need for times of prayer, perhaps in response to the preaching of the Word, when we can collectively cry out to God in prayer and perhaps pray in tongues?

7

PAUL:
THE GIFT OF TONGUES

In the previous two chapters, I have argued that it is important to understand the polemical nature of Paul's words in 1 Corinthians 12-14 and the underlying concerns that shape them. When we approach this important passage from this fuller perspective, we find that Paul is more appreciative of the sign-value of tongues than is often recognized. His perspective fits together harmoniously with and complements the Spirit-inspired witness provided by Luke and by the author of the Long Ending of Mark. Additionally, when we read this passage with sensitivity to Paul's ultimate concerns, we also discover that Paul clearly highlights the edifying nature of glossolalia for the individual believer, affirms its availability to every believer, and recognizes its value, in special instances, for the entire church gathered together in corporate worship. We may summarize by saying that the New Testament, and Paul is a major contributor here, highlights three ways in which speaking in tongues serves to encourage and edify individual Christians and the Christian community: (1) Tongues serve as a dramatic, observable sign of God's powerful presence in our midst and his call upon our lives; (2) Tongues are a powerful means by which the Spirit energizes our prayer and praise; and finally (3) Tongues, in a manner similar to prophecy, can be the means by which the Holy Spirit speaks to the larger body through the inspired utterances of individual believers. In previous chapters I have highlighted the way in which glossolalia functions as a sign. In this chapter I will explain in more detail how speaking in tongues functions as an aid to our prayer life and how it can function in group settings as a form of proclamation. Let us begin by examining what Paul has to say about praying and singing 'in the Spirit'.

Tongues as Prayer

Paul begins his discussion of spiritual gifts in 1 Corinthians 12-14 with a striking statement. He reminds the Corinthians of their pagan past: 'You know that when you were pagans, somehow or other you were influenced and led astray to mute idols' (1 Cor. 12.2). Paul here echoes the Old Testament's repudiation of the folly of worshipping objects made by human hands. Psalm 115.5, which drips with irony, illustrates the theme well, 'They have mouths, but cannot speak, eyes, but they cannot see'.

Paul then shifts the focus from the pagan past to the Christian present. The reference to 'mute idols' stands in stark contrast to the Corinthian Christians' present experience of God. The God who has so beautifully and concretely revealed himself in Christ continues to speak through the Holy Spirit. Paul reminds the Corinthians that God is truly speaking in and through them when the Holy Spirit inspires praise to Jesus in their midst. Paul declares, '… no one can say, "Jesus is Lord", except by the Holy Spirit' (1 Cor. 12.3).

Paul's instruction on the gifts of the Spirit that follows (1 Corinthians 12-14) is, in reality, a continuation of this theme. The God who speaks and acts through the inspiration of the Holy Spirit is the transcendent God who longs for relationship, who 'is not far from each one of us', and who has revealed himself supremely in Jesus (Acts 17.24-31). This God, the one true God, speaks.

One of the ways that God speaks is through prayers inspired by the Holy Spirit. As we have noted, these prayers sometimes take the form of glossolalia. Paul refers to this kind of prayer when he describes the ability to speak in 'different kinds of tongues' (γένη γλωσσῶν; 1 Cor. 12.10) as one of the 'gifts' (χαρισμάτων; 1 Cor. 12.4) of the Spirit. Paul frequently uses the phrase, λαλέω γλώσσαις ('to speak in tongues'), when he refers to this gift.[1]

---

[1] 1 Corinthians 12.30; 13.1; 14.2, 4, 6, 13, 18, 23, 27, 39.

It should be noted that this phrase, λαλέω γλώσσαις ('to speak in tongues'), typically refers to unintelligible utterances inspired by the Holy Spirit. This is certainly the case for Paul.[2] According to Paul, tongues must be interpreted if they are to be understood (1 Cor. 14.6-19, 28; cf. 12.10, 30). The one who speaks in tongues 'does not speak to men but to God' and 'utters mysteries' by the Spirit (1 Cor. 14.2). Paul also declares, 'If I pray in a tongue, my spirit prays, but my mind is unfruitful' (1 Cor. 14.14). Furthermore, according to Paul, these unintelligible 'tongues' typically do not take the form of unknown human languages (xenolalia). This is evident from Paul's usage throughout this passage, 1 Corinthians 12-14. Paul does not countenance the possibility that someone with an acquired knowledge of the 'tongue' spoken might be present and able to interpret. On the contrary, Paul insists that one can interpret these tongues only if one has a special gift of the Spirit to do so (1 Cor. 12.10). For this reason a number of commentators have suggested that Paul considered the gift of tongues to be the miraculous ability to speak the languages of the angels (1 Cor. 13.1).[3] In 1 Corinthians 13.1 the phrase, 'the tongues of men and angels', most likely refers to two kinds of spontaneous, Spirit-inspired speech. Here Paul appears to link the former with prophecy and the latter with 'speaking in tongues' or glossolalia. All of this indicates that when Paul refers to the gift of tongues or speaking in tongues, typically he does not have xenolalia in mind. Quite the contrary, with these phrases Paul refers to spontaneous utterances inspired by the Holy Spirit that are unintelligible to both the speaker and the hearer.

At this point, many may be tempted to ask, then why speak in tongues? What is the value of speaking words that no one understands? That is the question that I wish to address in the pages that follow. Let us begin our answer by examining Paul's attitude toward tongues in 1 Corinthians 12-14.

Paul's Attitude Toward Tongues

Even a casual reading of 1 Corinthians 12-14 reveals an obvious fact: all was not well in the church at Corinth. The Christians at

---

[2] We have noted that the only instance of xenolalia in the New Testament is found in Acts 2.

[3] See, for example, Mark Stibbe, *Know Your Spiritual Gifts: Practising the Presents of God* (London: Marshall Pickering, 1997), p. 156.

Corinth exhibited a serious lack of understanding concerning the purpose and use of spiritual gifts. This in turn had a significantly negative impact on their corporate gatherings. Their misuse of spiritual gifts was creating divisions within the church and unnecessarily alienating others outside the church.

The problems at Corinth, at least with reference to their corporate worship, centered on their misunderstanding and abuse of the gift of tongues. As we have noted, the Corinthians exhibited a remarkable lack of concern for intelligibility in their meetings. So, Paul reminds them that one who speaks in tongues 'utters mysteries' (1 Cor. 14.2) and does not edify others (1 Cor. 14.4). And he asks, 'unless you speak intelligible words with your tongue, how will anyone know what you are saying?' (1 Cor. 14.9). Finally, Paul urges them to 'stop thinking like children' (1 Cor. 14.20). He insists that tongues should not eclipse proclamation or instruction (1 Cor. 14.23-25). Paul then concludes with a command. 'If anyone speaks in a tongue … someone must interpret' (1 Cor. 14.27).

The Corinthians' abuse of tongues, however, flowed from an even more disturbing source. We have noted that at least one faction at Corinth viewed speaking in tongues as a means of establishing their superior status. Speaking in tongues offered them a means by which they might display their authority and power over others in the church. Of course Paul seeks to correct this immature and destructive mindset. He does so by highlighting the rich variety of God's gracious gifts (1 Cor. 12.4-6). Paul declares that everyone has a role to play in corporate worship (1 Cor. 12.11-27) and that edification is the overriding goal (1 Cor. 12.7). Ultimately, Paul's argument reaches rhetorical heights with his call to exercise love. 'If I speak in tongues … but have not love, I am only a resounding gong or a clanging cymbal' (1 Cor. 13.1).

All of this is clear, but it is not the full picture. Unfortunately, many Christians today miss this point. They simply gloss over the surface, read Paul's polemical language, and dismiss tongues as an exotic aberration, an immature and emotional response that is at best outdated and often damaging and divisive. These negative perceptions have been reinforced by various psychological studies from a previous generation that merely parroted already established presuppositions. Although the spurious methodologies and dubious conclusions of these early studies have been discredited by more recent and credible research,[4] the negative stereotypes these studies fostered die hard.

It is important to read Paul's polemic against the abuse of tongues in 1 Corinthians 12-14 with two additional strands of biblical evidence in mind. First, we must recognize that Paul criticizes the abuse of tongues, not the gift itself.[5] This explains why Paul shows such remarkable restraint in his teaching on gifts of the Spirit in general and speaking in tongues in particular. In view of the problems in Corinth, Paul's words at the very beginning of this letter to the church are truly astonishing. Paul writes,

> I always thank God for you because of his grace given you in Christ Jesus. For in him you have been enriched in every way — in all your speaking and in all your knowledge — because our testimony about Christ was confirmed in you. Therefore you do not lack any spiritual gift as you eagerly wait for our Lord Jesus Christ to be revealed (1 Cor. 1.4-7).

Thus, at the outset of his epistle, Paul unequivocally affirms the divine origin and the potentially rich impact of the very gifts that were causing the greatest problems in the church. That this is not merely some rhetorical strategy to win over the Corinthians becomes clear when we take a close look at Paul's instruction in 1 Corinthians 12-14. Although Paul clearly seeks to correct erroneous views and practice, Paul will not deny the validity of tongues nor will he denigrate the gift's value. Actually, Paul is quite positive concerning tongues when the gift is used for the right reasons and in the appropriate setting. Paul affirms that the private manifestation of tongues is edifying to the speaker (1 Cor. 14.5) and, in an autobiographical note, he thanks God for the frequent manifestation of tongues in his private prayer-life (1 Cor. 14.18). Fearful that his instructions to the Corinthians concerning the proper use of tongues 'in the assembly' might be misunderstood, he explicitly commands them not to forbid speaking in tongues (1 Cor. 14.39). And, with

---

[4] Max Turner states, 'Contrary to earlier claims, there is no evidence that "tongues speech" is correlated with low intellect, education, social position or pathological psychology' (*The Holy Spirit and Spiritual Gifts: Then and Now* [Carlisle, UK: Paternoster, 1996], p. 305). See also the numerous studies he cites.

[5] Craig S. Keener, *Gift & Giver: The Holy Spirit for Today* (Grand Rapids: Baker, 2001), p. 107.

reference to the private manifestation of tongues, Paul declares, 'I would like every one of you to speak in tongues ...' (1 Cor. 14.5).

Let us now return to the question posed earlier, why should we speak words that no one understands? How does speaking in tongues enrich us 'in every way'? The answer lies in Paul's description of speaking in tongues as a special form of prayer, a special form of communion with God. Here it is helpful to keep in mind the second strand of biblical data that helps us maintain a more balanced reading of Paul: numerous New Testament passages outside of 1 Corinthians, most of which were also written by Paul, add further perspective on this gift. These texts, in concert with Paul's teaching in 1 Corinthians 12-14, enable us to describe the nature of the gift of tongues in some detail. When we examine this biblical material, we find that the New Testament and Paul in particular present speaking in tongues as Spirit-inspired prayer that issues forth as either praise to God or intercession for us and through us.

Tongues as Praise
Paul describes speaking in tongues as a gift that functions in two distinct settings: the private and the communal. The Corinthian abuse of tongues took place during their meetings when they worshipped together. So, Paul challenges their improper attitudes and expression of tongues in these corporate settings. We shall examine Paul's teaching on the proper use of tongues in the corporate setting later (see Tongues as Proclamation below). Here, however, we want to examine what Paul's directives tell us about the private expression of this gift.

As we have noted, Paul is quite positive about the private expression of tongues. He explicitly states that tongues are edifying, that tongues 'builds up' the one speaking (1 Cor. 14.4). Paul's words here also help us begin to understand how this edification takes place. Paul declares that 'anyone who speaks in a tongue does not speak to men but to God' (1 Cor. 14.2). Indeed, the person speaking in tongues 'utters mysteries' by the Spirit (1 Cor. 14.2). While Paul can use the term 'mystery' (μυστήριον) to refer to specific aspects of God's redemptive plan (e.g. the inclusion of the Gentiles; Eph. 3.6), he uses the term in various ways. Here, the term simply 'carries ... the sense of that which lies outside the understanding, both for the speaker and the hearer'.[6] As Gordon Fee notes, this understanding of the term flows naturally from the fact that the speaker is addressing God. The content of specific mysteries pertaining to God's plan revealed by the Spirit would 'scarcely need to be spoken back to God'.[7] Paul's point is thus relatively simple: the person who speaks in tongues speaks words known only to God.

Two other important implications follow. Paul declares that these words, known only to God, are inspired by the Holy Spirit and they are addressed to God. Although the description of tongues as addressed 'not ... to men but to God' (1 Cor. 14.2) may highlight their unintelligibility (only God understands them) rather than their specific content (only praise addressed to God), there can be little doubt that Paul anticipates that the private expression of tongues will often take the form of praise directed to God. This understanding of tongues as doxological prayer is anticipated at the outset of Paul's discussion of spiritual gifts. While the idols are mute, the true God inspires praise to Jesus through the Holy Spirit (1 Cor. 12.3). Of course this inspired praise is often expressed with intelligible words, whether they be sung or proclaimed. Nevertheless, Paul here makes it clear that at times this praise will be expressed in words that are not understood (i.e. glossolalia).

1 Corinthians 14.14-17. This doxological understanding of tongues surfaces again later in Paul's argument. In 1 Cor. 14.14-17 Paul's primary objective is to persuade the Corinthians to emphasize intelligible discourse in their corporate meetings. So he declares,

> If I pray in a tongue, my spirit prays, but my mind is unfruitful. So what shall I do? I will pray with my spirit, but I will also pray with my mind; I will sing with my spirit, but I will also sing with my mind (1 Cor. 14.14-15).

The contrasts that Paul makes between praying and singing with 'my spirit' and with 'my mind' are instructive. First, it is evident that when Paul here speaks of praying with 'my spirit', the activity of the

---

[6] Fee, *First Corinthians*, p. 656.

[7] Fee, *First Corinthians*, p. 656.

Holy Spirit praying with or through his spirit is implied.[8] The larger context of 1 Corinthians 12-14 demands this (1 Cor. 12.7-11; 14.2, 16). Additionally, the contrast Paul offers with the terms 'my spirit' and 'my mind' highlights the important point noted above. When the Spirit produces glossolalic praise by praying with and through our spirit, our minds are not fully engaged; or, to put it simply, we do not understand what the Spirit is saying through us. Nevertheless, in spite of this lack of understanding, Paul affirms that as the Spirit prays through us, we are edified.

The fact that we are edified and enriched by this non-cognitive communion with God should not surprise us. The mystics and the contemplative tradition have highlighted this truth for centuries. I recall several years ago attending an early-morning prayer meeting at a theological institution. The leader of the session called for a long period of silence. In fact, almost all of our prayer time was spent in absolute silence. After the time of prayer ended, I spoke with the man who had led the session. I noted that I appreciated the period of silence, but wondered if they ever expressed their prayers with joyful shouts and loud declarations of praise as well. He thought for a moment and then responded, 'No, we follow the mystics and the contemplative tradition'. He added, 'The mystics felt that through silence we are able to experience God directly, in an unmediated way that transcends our rational faculties'. I smiled and then he began to smile too. He knew I was a Pentecostal and he anticipated my response. I replied, 'That is exactly how we Pentecostals describe our experience of speaking in tongues. When we speak in tongues, we experience God directly, in a way that transcends our cognitive processes. However, there is a difference. When we speak in tongues, it's rarely quiet. It's usually loud and joyful.'

I would add that we Pentecostals together with Paul do understand that there is an important, cognitive dimension to our faith and worship. This mystical experience of tongues is grounded in the gospel and biblical teaching. As a result, it is an experience that above all brings praise and glory to Jesus. If speaking in tongues for Paul and Pentecostals is a mystical experience, it is nonetheless an experience centered on Christ. Ulrich Luz, in his essay, 'Paul as

---

[8] In 1 Cor. 14.15 the Greek is ambiguous and can be translated 'pray with my spirit' or 'pray in the Spirit;' so also with the verb, 'sing'. Either way, the inspiration of the Holy Spirit is either implied or explicitly stated.

Mystic', states the matter well. He argues that the gift of the Spirit is the experiential basis of Paul's Christ-mysticism, which centers on 'the conformity of the believer with the Lord Jesus in his passion and in his resurrection glory'.[9] Luz notes that 'the fear and panic at "enthusiasm" and any *theologia gloriae* which marks out many Protestant theologians is unknown to Paul, for it is not a question of his own glory, but Christ's'.[10]

The Christ-centered nature of this charismatic experience becomes even more apparent as we examine further Paul's understanding of glossolalia as doxological prayer. Before we proceed, however, let us first summarize our argument up to this point. Paul affirms that glossolalia is speech inspired by the Holy Spirit. While the specific meaning of the words uttered is unknown to us, it is known to God. Indeed, these words typically take the form of praise directed to God. This doxological function of tongues is anticipated in 1 Cor. 12.2-3 and explicitly stated in 1 Cor. 14.14-17.

In 1 Cor. 14.14-15 Paul refers to praying and singing with his spirit, which undoubtedly takes place through the inspiration of the Holy Spirit. As we have seen, the context, 'For if I pray in a tongue …' (v. 14), and the 'spirit' and 'mind' contrast, indicate that this Spirit-inspired type of praying (προσεύξομαι τῷ πνεύματι) and singing (ψαλῶ τῷ πνεύματι) is, in reality, praying in tongues and singing in tongues.

Paul describes the nature of this praying and singing in tongues further in 1 Cor. 14.16-17. In v. 16 he refers to this praying and singing in tongues as praise directed to God ('If you are praising God with your spirit …').[11] Then, in the next verse, Paul describes this Spirit-inspired glossolalia as a means of giving thanks, 'You may be giving thanks well enough …' (1 Cor. 14.17). Although Paul does not elaborate here further since his chief concern lies elsewhere, these verses indicate that Paul understands praying and singing in tongues (literally, praying [προσεύξομαι τῷ πνεύματι] and

[9] Ulrich Luz, 'Paul as Mystic', in Graham N. Stanton, Bruce W. Longenecker, and Stephen C. Barton (eds.), *The Holy Spirit and Christian Origins: Essays in Honor of James D.G. Dunn* (Grand Rapids: Eerdmans, 2004), p. 140.

[10] Luz, 'Paul as Mystic', p. 141.

[11] Again, the Greek text is ambiguous here. 1 Corinthians 14.16 can be rendered, 'If you are praising God with your spirit …' or 'If you are praising God in the Spirit …'

singing [ψαλῶ τῷ πνεύματι] in the Spirit) as a charismatic form of thanksgiving and praise.

Ephesians 6.18. This understanding of tongues as doxological prayer is affirmed in several other Pauline passages. In Eph. 6.18, immediately after encouraging his readers 'to take the sword of the Spirit' (v. 17), Paul urges them to 'pray in the Spirit [προσευχό-μενοι ... ἐν πνεύματι] on all occasions with all kinds of prayers and requests'. James Dunn's paraphrase of this verse is helpful, '... in every specific situation hold yourselves open to the prayer of the Spirit'.[12] The wording here is almost identical with 1 Cor. 14.15. Both verses speak of 'praying in the Spirit' (προσεύχομαι ἐν/τῷ πνεύματι). This suggests that in Eph. 6.18 Paul's exhortation to engage in charismatic prayer includes the notion of praying in tongues even if it is not restricted exclusively to it. The fact that Paul urges the Ephesians to pray 'on all occasions' or 'at all times', an exhortation that is repeated in the second half of the verse ('With this in mind, be alert and always keep on praying for all the saints' [Eph. 6.18]), suggests that Paul here is speaking broadly of sponta-neous, Spirit-inspired prayer. In Paul's mind, this kind of prayer likely included glossolalic prayer as well as intelligible forms of praise, intercession, and petition. This wider perspective is probably also implied with the phrase 'with all kinds of prayers and requests' (Eph. 6.18). The thought of intercession is clearly foremost in Paul's mind in the latter part of the verse, but the initial exhortation is broad and would appear to include praise and thanksgiving as well.

Jude 20. The exhortation to 'pray in the Spirit' also appears in a non-Pauline passage, Jude 20. In Jude 20 we read, 'But you, dear friends, build yourselves up in your most holy faith and pray in the Holy Spirit (ἐν πνεύματι ἁγίῳ προσευχόμενοι)'. Jude was writ-ten by the brother of Jesus (and James) in the late 50s or early 60s CE. Jude wrote to combat false teachers who had misappropriated Paul's teaching on grace by taking it to unhealthy extremes.[13] These false teachers claimed to have the Holy Spirit, but Jude insists that they merely 'follow their natural instincts and do not have the Spirit'

---

[12] Dunn, *Jesus and the Spirit*, p. 239.

[13] Gene L. Green, *Jude and 2 Peter* (ECNT; Grand Rapids: Baker Academic, 2008), pp. 17-18.

(Jude 19).[14] In Jude 20 the false teachers' lack of the Spirit is contrasted with the Spirit-inspired quality of the prayers of the brothers and sisters in the church. The language that Jude uses here, 'pray in the Holy Spirit', parallels closely Paul's usage in 1 Cor. 14.15-16 and Eph. 6.18. Thus, as Towner and Harvey observe, 'there is a strong consensus that here Jude means prayer in a Spirit-given tongue (glossolalia)'.[15]

Praying in the Spirit here is described as a means of building yourself up 'in your most holy faith'. How does this edification take place? The context of Jude and the way in which this charismatic prayer is described elsewhere in the New Testament suggest that there are at least three ways that Spirit-inspired glossolalia 'builds up' the one who prays.

First, as we have seen so clearly in Acts, praying in tongues strengthens the believers' sense of connection with the apostolic faith. More specifically, in this instance, glossolalia serves as a dramatic, tangible sign (both for the individual and the community), over against the false teachers, that they are indeed the true people of God.

Additionally, I would add that the Spirit builds us up in our most holy faith by interceding through us and for us (Rom. 8.26-27). In the midst of our weakness, the Spirit prays for us. This is a theme that we will develop below.

Finally, as the Spirit prays through the believers, there is also a strong sense of communion with Christ. This is expressed beautifully in the Abba prayer of Rom. 8.15-16 and Gal. 4.6, and implied in 1 Corinthians (cf. 12.3; 14.2, 14-17). Paul declares that 'the Spirit himself testifies with our spirit that we are God's children' (Rom. 8.16). Although the Abba prayer probably describes charismatic prayer more broadly, it undoubtedly includes glossolalic prayer.[16] Furthermore, it paints a powerful picture of what happens as the

---

[14] According to Harvey and Towner, the term 'dreamers' (Jude 8) suggests that the false teachers laid claim to prophetic and visionary revelation (Robert Harvey and Philip H. Towner, *2 Peter and Jude* [IVP; Downers Grove, IL: Inter-Varsity Press, 2009], p. 196).

[15] Harvey and Towner, *Jude*, p. 225. So also Dunn, *Jesus and the Spirit*, pp. 245-46 and Richard J. Bauckham, *Jude, 2 Peter* (WBC 50; Waco, TX: Word, 1983), p. 113, both describe the prayer as 'charismatic prayer' which includes glossolalia.

[16] That is to say, on occasion the Abba prayer may be expressed through speaking in tongues.

Spirit prays through us. We are caught up in the love of Christ and filled with joy as we begin to glimpse in part the wonder of our adoption as God's children. Somehow the Holy Spirit reveals a bit of the majesty and wonder of God's grace to us as he prays through us. No wonder that we are caught up in spiritual rapture and that human words fail to adequately express what we feel.[17] No wonder that as the Spirit prays through us and declares 'the wonders of God' (Acts 2.11; cf. 1 Cor. 14.16-17) that he reverts to his vernacular, the language of heaven.

This last point serves to remind us of the beauty and transforming power of worship. As we give praise and thanks to God, our perspective is changed. Our weakness and struggles seem to fade away as we are ushered into the presence of a mighty and powerful God. Certainly every encounter with God, every experience of worship that is centered on Christ is energized by the Holy Spirit. Nevertheless, Paul and the early church understood that our worship is often energized in a special way by the Holy Spirit. These spontaneous moments of spiritual rapture are described with the phrase 'in the Spirit'.[18] These wonderful experiences often include glossolalic praise.

1 Thessalonians 5.19. In 1 Thess. 5.16-22 Paul alludes to this kind of charismatic experience. He offers the church at Thessalonica a series of exhortations. He urges them on with these words: 'Be joyful always; pray continually; give thanks in all circumstances, for this is God's will for you in Christ Jesus' (1 Thess. 5.16-18). These exhortations apply primarily to individual believers and are expressed daily in the midst of the diverse challenges and situations that each person faces. Then, I would argue, Paul shifts his attention to the Thessalonians' community life. He issues a series of commands that are designed to enhance their corporate worship, which in turn will enable individual Christians to embrace the personal exhortations he has just delivered. Paul's instructions for their 'life together' are as follows: 'Do not put out the Spirit's fire; do not treat prophecies

---

[17] Robert Graves echoes this thought when he queries, how can we 'possibly express those ineffable feelings that well up from time to time within our innermost beings?' (Graves, *Praying in the Spirit* [Old Tappan, NJ: Chosen Books, 1987], p. 63).

[18] So also Bauckham, *Jude*, p. 113, who cites numerous NT texts including Lk. 2.27; 4.1; Acts 19.21; and 1 Cor. 12.3 among others.

with contempt. Test everything. Hold on to the good. Avoid every kind of evil' (1 Thess. 5.19-22).

The structure of Paul's words at this point are instructive. Notice how Paul juxtaposes, 'do not put out the Spirit's fire', with 'do not treat prophecies with contempt'. Paul's wording at this point is reminiscent of his coupling of tongues and prophecy in 1 Cor. 14.39, where he declares, 'be eager to prophesy, and do not forbid speaking in tongues'. Indeed, this verse forms a striking parallel to 1 Thess. 5.19-20. Of course the close association between prophecy and tongues is characteristic of the book of Acts as well. Tongues and prophecy are explicitly linked in Acts 19.6, and by implication in Acts 2.16-18 and Acts 10.43-46. All of this suggests that when Paul encourages his readers to 'not put out the Spirit's fire', he has speaking in tongues specifically in mind.[19]

This conclusion in turn suggests that speaking in tongues, like prophecy, may assist us in our quest to 'be joyful always' and aid us as we seek to 'pray continually' and 'give thanks in all circumstances' (1 Thess. 5.16-18). The larger context of Paul's epistles indicates that this is very much in line with Paul's teaching elsewhere (cf. 1 Cor. 14.15-17; Eph. 5.18-20; 6.18). When we see that tongues is, above all, Spirit-inspired doxological prayer, the connections Paul draws between speaking in tongues and joyful prayer and thanksgiving are entirely understandable.

Ephesians 5.18 and Colossians 3.16. In addition to 1 Cor. 12.2-3, 14.14-17, Eph. 6.18, Jude 20, and 1 Thess. 5.19, two other passages present speaking in tongues as a form of doxological prayer.[20] In Eph. 5.18 Paul admonishes his readers not to get drunk on wine; instead, he declares, 'be filled with the Spirit'. In the verses that follow (Eph. 5.18-21), Paul uses a series of participles to describe what this imperative means. To be filled with the Spirit, then, involves: (1) 'speaking' to one another with psalms, hymns, and spiritual songs' (v. 19a); (2) 'singing' and 'making music' in your heart to the Lord (v. 19b); (3) 'giving thanks' always to God the Father in the

---

[19] So also J.P.M. Sweet, 'A Sign for Unbelievers: Paul's Attitude to Glossolalia', in Watson E. Mills (ed.), *Speaking in Tongues: A Guide to Research on Glossolalia* (Grand Rapids: Eerdmans, 1986), p. 153.

[20] Of course Acts 2.11 and 10.46 (and implicitly 19.6) could be added to this list, but we have already discussed these passages in previous chapters.

name of our Lord Jesus Christ for everything (v. 20); and (4) 'sub-mitting' to one another out of reverence for Christ (v. 21).

The initial phrase in Eph. 5.19 cited above is especially important for our study. Paul exhorts the Ephesian believers to 'speak to one another with psalms, hymns and spiritual songs (ᾠδαῖς πνευματικαῖς)' (Eph. 5.19). We find another close parallel to this passage in Col. 3.16. There Paul encourages his readers with these words: 'Let the word of Christ dwell in you richly as you teach and admonish one another with all wisdom, and as you sing psalms, hymns and spiritual songs [ᾠδαῖς πνευματικαῖς] with gratitude in your hearts to God' (Col. 3.16). The Greek phrase translated, 'psalms, hymns, and spiritual songs', in both texts is virtually identical.

As James Dunn notes, these texts, in concert with 1 Cor. 14.15, demonstrate that 'Paul recognizes a kind of charismatic hymnody – both a singing in tongues … and a singing with intelligible words'.[21] There are indeed several indications that point to the fact that Paul views this charismatic hymnody as inclusive of speaking in tongues. First, as we have noted, the contrast in 1 Cor. 14.15 between singing 'with my spirit' and singing 'with my mind' clearly distinguishes between singing in tongues on the one hand, and singing with intelligible words on the other. So, here, in this text, Paul unambiguously refers to singing in tongues as a form of charismatic thanksgiving and praise (cf. 1 Cor. 14.16-17). Secondly, there is a spontaneity and obvious charismatic quality that is implied in both the contrast between being drunk with wine and being filled with the Spirit (Eph. 5.18) and the vocabulary employed in Col. 3.16 ('word of God', 'in all wisdom', and 'with grace').[22] Finally, the adjective that qualifies the third type of singing named in both lists, 'spiritual' (πνευματ-ικαῖς), suggests that Paul here, like in 1 Cor. 14.15, is again speaking about different kinds of charismatic singing: intelligible (psalms and hymns) and unintelligible or glossolalic songs (spiritual songs).[23] Since the term 'spiritual' (πνευματικαῖς) derives from the word, 'Spirit' (πνεῦμα), the term 'spiritual song' is essentially a reference

---

[21] Dunn, *Jesus and the Spirit*, p. 238.

[22] This point is made by Dunn, *Jesus and the Spirit*, p. 238.

[23] If 'spiritual' qualifies all three categories of songs, then all three would refer to charismatic singing and embrace both intelligible and glossolalic expressions.

to singing 'in the Spirit'. We have already noted that in the early church this phrase, 'in the Spirit', becomes virtually a technical term for charismatic inspiration and typically includes glossolalia.

These references to singing in tongues highlight once again the fact that Paul understands speaking in tongues as doxological prayer, a Spirit-inspired form of praise and thanksgiving. In Col. 3.16 Paul suggests that the 'spiritual songs' should be sung 'with gratitude' and directed to God. These 'spiritual songs' are also understood to be a source of encouragement for the entire community (cf. 'admonish one another'). We probably should also understand the phrases that qualify what it means to be 'filled with the Spirit' in Eph. 5.18-21 as interrelated. Thus, 'speaking' to one another in spiritual songs is not unrelated to 'singing' to the Lord, 'giving thanks' to God, and 'submitting' to one another. Together these activities all enhance corporate praise and the life of the community. In short, here we have references to corporate 'singing in tongues' that are edifying to the body of believers and glorifying to God. This is, of course, what we would expect when we begin to understand that singing in tongues, like speaking in tongues, represents a spontaneous, Spirit-inspired expression of love and devotion to the triune God, the God who has supremely and wonderfully revealed himself in Jesus.

Tongues as Intercession

Paul not only presents speaking and singing in tongues as a form of praise and thanksgiving to God, he also describes tongues as a means of intercessory prayer. This is perhaps nowhere more clearly expressed than in Rom. 8.26. In Romans 8 Paul seeks to encourage his readers by helping them understand that our present experience of the Holy Spirit is a foretaste of the glorious future salvation that we await. Although we struggle with the fact that now we only experience this glorious 'life of the future' in part (8.23), we can be encouraged by the fact that the Holy Spirit is presently at work in our lives, transforming us into the people that God has called us to be (8.9-13) and enabling us to share rich fellowship with God in Christ (8.14-17). In fact, our present experience of the Spirit is so rich, it serves as a testimony to us that God will consummate his redemptive plan; and when he does, we will experience the full richness of his blessings, including the transformation of our bodies and intimate fellowship with him (8.23, 39).

Paul refers to our present experience of the Holy Spirit in Rom. 8.16. He declares that we are moved to cry, 'Abba, Father', because 'the Spirit himself testifies with our spirit that we are God's children' (8.16). This leads Paul to declare, 'I consider that our present sufferings are not worth comparing with the glory that will be revealed in us' (8.18). This suffering, this longing for God's full redemption, is experienced by all of creation. So, Paul observes, 'We know that the whole creation has been groaning as in the pains of childbirth right up to the present time' (8.22). However, Paul emphasizes that this struggle is one that is felt on the personal level as well as the cosmic, 'Not only so, but we ourselves, who have the firstfruits of the Spirit, groan inwardly as we wait eagerly for our adoption as sons, the redemption of our bodies' (8.23).

In this gripping description of the tension that we face as Christians – as people who experience inwardly and see outwardly on a daily basis the transforming power of the Holy Spirit at work in the midst of sin, death, and decay – Paul reminds us once again that we are not alone (cf. Rom. 8.16, 23). He declares that we do not face the inevitable struggles that mark this 'already/not yet' tension on our own. No, 'the Spirit helps us in our weakness' (8.26). Paul continues,

> We do not know what we ought to pray for, but the Spirit himself intercedes for us with groans that words cannot express. And he who searches our hearts knows the mind of the Spirit, because the Spirit intercedes for the saints in accordance with God's will (Rom. 8.26-27).

This is a stirring picture. Although we often do not know what or even how to pray, the Spirit prays through us, and in the process inspires words that sound like inarticulate groans. The Spirit's prayers, although unintelligible to us, are filled with meaning, for they represent God's own intercession on behalf of his people. Romans 8.27 echoes the earlier reference to intercession in v. 26 and might be paraphrased in this way, 'He, that is the Spirit, who searches our hearts, knows what is spiritual, and thus he intercedes for the saints according to God's plan'.

Two lines of argumentation suggest that Paul here has glossolalia primarily, though perhaps not exclusively, in view.[24] The first set of arguments are linked to the immediate context; the second, to the larger context of Paul's epistle to the Romans.

The immediate context highlights the fact that these 'groans', like the Abba cry of Rom. 8.15, are: actual utterances inspired by the Spirit; that these utterances flow from an intimate encounter with God rather than a rational apprehension of specific truths; and these utterances are especially powerful and meaningful because the speaker recognizes that in some amazing way, 'God is speaking in and through me'.

It goes without saying that when Paul declares that by the Spirit 'we cry, "Abba, Father"' (Rom. 8.15), he has in mind actual utterances. If the believers at Rome had no experience of this sort of cry, then Paul's words would make little sense and have no value. The same must be said of the Spirit-inspired 'groans' of Rom. 8.26. Paul is clearly referring here to charismatic manifestations, spontaneous utterances inspired by the Holy Spirit that his readers have actually experienced. In other words, Paul is appealing to experiences that he and the Christians at Rome share.[25] The fact that Paul can make such appeals should remind us that this kind of charismatic experience was not rare but rather the norm for the early church. Of course, our survey of the New Testament documents has already established this fact.

We should also note that these utterances were undoubtedly articulated and typically loud. Dunn notes that the verb Paul uses when he describes the Abba cry, κράζειν ('to cry out', Rom. 8.15, Gal. 4.6), 'is a very strong one'. It generally means 'to cry out loudly', and thus is used for the 'screams and shrieks of demoniacs' (e.g. Mk 5.5; 9.26; Lk. 9.39). Dunn concludes that the context of Rom.

---

[24] Frank D. Macchia notes a string of ancient and modern scholars who interpret the 'groans' of Rom. 8.26 as a reference to glossolalia (Macchia, 'Sighs Too Deep for Words: Toward a Theology of Glossolalia', *JPT* 1 [1992], p. 59).

[25] So also Gordon Fee, *God's Empowering Presence: The Holy Spirit in the Letters of Paul* (Peabody, MA: Hendrickson, 1994), pp. 577-78, 584 and Ernst Käsemann, who also highlights this fact and states that 'the place of these sighs must rather be … the church's assembly for worship' ('Cry for Liberty in the Church's Worship', in Käsemann, *Perspectives on Paul* [Philadelphia: Fortress Press, 1971], p. 129).

8.15 and Gal. 4.6 suggests κράζειν in these verses is 'a cry of some intensity, probably a loud cry, and perhaps ... an ecstatic cry'.[26]

The same can be said of the 'groans' of Rom. 8.26. Similar Greek terms (forms of the verb, στενάζω, or the noun, στεναγμός) are used to describe the groaning of creation in Rom. 8.22, the groans of believers who have 'the firstfruits of the Spirit' in Rom. 8.23, and the groans prompted by the intercession of the Spirit in Rom. 8.26. The fact that Paul can speak of 'the whole creation ... groaning as in the pains of childbirth' (Rom. 8.22) should make it abundantly clear that these are not silent sighs or quiet murmurings. No, Paul is describing with these words loud utterances, utterances known and shared by the congregation, utterances inspired by the Spirit that have marked their worship and their prayers.

Paul suggests that these utterances are not only vocalized and loud, but that they issue from a deep, intimate encounter with God. Paul declares, 'The Spirit himself testifies with our spirit that we are God's children' (Rom. 8.16). What relational bond can be stronger than that of parents to their child? This incredible sense of relationship, of confidence before God, is the source of the Abba cry. And it is not simply understood; rather, it is felt. Just as a small infant knows intuitively that she is loved by her parents, so also we know that we are 'heirs of God and co-heirs with Christ' (Rom. 8.17). We know this because we experience the reality, the fruit of this relationship, through the work of the Holy Spirit in our hearts. When we do, as Paul and the Romans testify, occasionally this remarkable realization will erupt in joyful, Spirit-inspired speech.

Paul also envisions another kind of realization that will produce charismatic speech. This is the realization of our utter weakness that he describes so vividly in Rom. 8.18-27. We long for the completion of the process that began with our repentance and faith in Christ. We long for the transformation that is hinted at by the presence and leading of the Holy Spirit in our lives. We long to see Christ face to face. And yet we know that we cannot even begin to express the longings and desires that the Spirit has birthed within us. We know that we are incapable of fathoming the depths of God's love, the majesty of his holiness, or the wonder of his redemptive plan. We do not even know how to pray for our own needs, let alone those

---

[26] Dunn, *Jesus and the Spirit*, p. 240.

of our friends. Yet, just as we are overwhelmed by the realization of our utter weakness, the Spirit begins to pray through us. Even though we do not know how to pray, the Spirit intercedes for us and through us, utilizing words that transcend our ability to comprehend. Nevertheless, even as we speak in this inarticulate manner, even though our speech reflects our yearning and sounds like 'groans' (cf. 2 Cor. 5.1-4), we sense that something remarkable is taking place. We sense that God is speaking through us. It is this incredible awareness – this recognition that somehow God is present in our weakness and accomplishing through us that which we cannot comprehend but sense to be precisely what we need – that makes the groans of Rom. 8.26 so edifying and so special. So, it is to a charismatic manifestation marking our weakness that Paul appeals. Here he and the Christians at Rome stand on common ground.

All of this indicates that Paul has in mind spontaneous, Spirit-inspired utterances (i.e. charismatic speech) when he speaks of our 'groans' prompted by the Spirit. I would suggest, however, that we can say more. We have already noted that Paul's descriptions of the Abba cry and our inarticulate groans draw upon common, shared experiences. His words carry little meaning unless they describe experiences known and recognized by the believers at Rome. The one charismatic experience that fits Paul's description of inarticulate groans, that is cited in numerous New Testament documents, and that thus was clearly well known and established in the early church, is speaking in tongues.[27]

Many scholars have rejected this interpretation, arguing that since Paul in Romans 8 speaks of an experience of the Spirit that is common to every Christian, 'glossolalia can at most be in the background'.[28] Yet this judgment misses the fact, as we have noted, that for Paul speaking in tongues can be experienced by every believer. Furthermore, it is predicated on the erroneous assumption that speaking in tongues was a rather rare and exotic experience for the early church. We have established that there is ample evidence to challenge this view.

---

[27] So also Ernst Käsemann, *Commentary on Romans* (Grand Rapids: Eerdmans, 1980), p. 241.

[28] Sweet, 'Glossolalia', p. 152.

Other scholars have also questioned whether Paul has tongues in mind here because the term, στεναγμοῖς ἀλαλήτοις or 'groans that words cannot express' (Rom. 8.26), does not seem to mesh well with Paul's understanding of tongues as a language, albeit a heavenly language, one that we do not understand.[29] The judgment that Paul views speaking in tongues as an actual language is grounded in two facts: this is the normal sense of the term, γλῶσσα ('tongue'); and Paul's reference to a gift of interpretation (1 Cor. 12.10, 30) seems to demand it. While I agree that Paul does view speaking in tongues as a language (probably angelic, certainly heavenly rather human), I have trouble seeing this judgment as standing in conflict with Paul's reference to tongues as 'groans' in Rom. 8.26. Surely to suggest otherwise is a classic example of over exegesis. Paul here is not speaking as a linguist; rather, he speaks as one who shares this dramatic, powerful experience with the Christians at Rome. The similarities between speaking in tongues and 'groans' were for Paul and his readers (as they are for those familiar with tongues today) so vivid and clear that they do not require explanation.

Still others point to the fact that Paul does not specifically mention speaking in tongues in his gift list in Rom. 12.6-8. This would suggest, in their view, that Paul's Roman readers were not so familiar with tongues and would not have understood this allusion.[30] Yet this argument from silence is particularly weak. It may well be that Paul does not explicitly refer to tongues in Romans 12 or the rest of his epistle because this gift was well known to these believers and not abused or the source of a problem. There is, however, one other possibility that we must consider.

One other line of evidence lends support to our contention that Paul has glossolalia in mind when he speaks of the Spirit interceding for us and through us with inarticulate groans (Rom. 8.26). Although Paul does not have first hand knowledge of the church in Rome, he seems to be aware of at least the potential for trouble. His exhortations to the weak and to the strong in Rom. 14.1-15.6 and his warnings in Rom. 16.17-20 suggest that disagreements were

---

[29] See, for example, A.J.M. Wedderburn, 'Romans 8.26 – Towards a Theology of Glossolalia', *SJT* 28 (1975), p. 373.

[30] So also Dunn, *Jesus and the Spirit*, p. 241, who concludes that while the reference to inarticulate groans in Rom. 8.26 does not exclude glossolalia, it is not confined to it.

ready to boil over. A number of passages indicate that, 'a group in Rome shared at least some of the attitudes and values of the Corinthian gnostics'.[31] More specifically, this group probably advocated an over-realized eschatology that shared many points of contact with the problematic views that caused so much trouble in Corinth (cf. 1 Cor. 15.12).[32] The group at Corinth taught that they had already experienced a 'spiritual' resurrection and were thus fully 'mature'. It is, indeed, quite likely that a group in Rome advocated these views as well. Additionally, the Corinthian group, as we have noted, viewed speaking in tongues as a sign of their exalted, spiritual status. It is not without reason, then, that we suggest that the faction at Rome, like the one at Corinth, viewed speaking in tongues in this inappropriate manner as well.

If this was the case, then we can see why Paul would remind the church at Rome that speaking in tongues, far from being a sign that they had already received the fullness of 'salvation', was rather a sign of their weakness and expressed their yearning for the fullness of redemption, which we still await. This sign of yearning for our future, full redemption beautifully parallels and adds balance to the Abba cry, which is a sign of our present, though partial, experience of God's glorious inheritance. In short, Paul's language in Rom. 8.26, where he pictures speaking in tongues as Spirit-inspired groans, may well have highlighted a much needed and important theological truth. Ernst Käsemann puts it well, 'what enthusiasts regard as proof of their glorification [Paul] sees as sign of a lack'.[33]

This truth, I would add, not only speaks to the church at Rome, but also to our contemporary situation. Contemporary Pentecostals and charismatics also need to recognize that speaking in tongues is not a sign of our 'maturity' or our 'strength'. Although we do with good reason celebrate the present-ness of God's Kingdom, we must acknowledge that it has not yet fully 'arrived'. And neither have we. Quite the contrary, our groaning serves to remind us of our utter

---

[31] Dunn, *Jesus and the Spirit*, p. 268. He cites Rom. 6.1 and 1 Cor. 5-6; Rom. 13.13 and 1 Cor. 11.17-22; Rom. 14.1-15.6 and 1 Corinthians 8, 10.23-33; Rom. 16.17-18 and 1 Corinthians 1-4.

[32] Dunn asserts that Paul uses guarded language in Romans 6.4-5 when he speaks about the resurrection and in this way highlights that 'our participation in Christ's resurrection is still outstanding and future' (*Jesus and the Spirit*, p. 268).

[33] Käsemann, *Romans*, p. 241.

dependence on and need for God. Speaking in tongues is a symptom of our weakness, a manifestation of our yearning for that
which we have been promised but have not yet received. Yet here is
the beauty of this incredible experience. In the midst of our weakness, the Spirit himself intercedes through us on our behalf. In so
doing, the Spirit reveals to us a bit of the life of the future. He also
reveals his desire to use those who are willing to acknowledge their
need and, in their desperation, eagerly come to him with open
hearts.

Tongues as Proclamation

It is by now abundantly clear that Paul values speaking in tongues as
a wonderful form of charismatic prayer. The Spirit delights to inspire spontaneous, glossolalic expressions of praise and thanksgiving. The Holy Spirit also assists us as we pray by interceding
through us. These prayers of intercession are also often expressed
through speaking in tongues as, moved by the Spirit, we utter inarticulate groans – sounds that carry no cognitive meaning for us, but
that are understood by God and incredibly edifying to us nonetheless.

In addition to this function of speaking in tongues as charismatic
prayer, Paul envisions tongues as blessing the church in another
way. Paul declares that speaking in tongues, when exercised in concert with the gift of interpretation, can be the vehicle through which
the Holy Spirit speaks to the larger church body. In this way
tongues with interpretation functions very much like prophecy. The
difference, however, is that in this instance, the message to the
church is issued first through an inspired, unintelligible utterance in
tongues. This 'message in tongues' is then followed by a Spirit-
inspired interpretation of this utterance that is proclaimed in the
vernacular of those present and thus understood by all.

Let's examine this gift more closely. Paul refers to the gift of 'interpretation' of tongues (using forms of the noun, ἑρμηνεία, or the
verb, ἑρμηνεύω) together with the gift of tongues on three occasions (1 Cor. 12.10, 30; 14.26). The noun, ἑρμηνεία, and the verb,
ἑρμηνεύω, do not appear very often in the New Testament or the
LXX. When they do, they most frequently refer to 'translation'.

However, the terms can be used more generally with the sense of 'explanation' or 'interpretation' (cf. Lk. 24.27).

We have already highlighted that fact that Paul understands speaking in tongues to refer to unintelligible, Spirit-inspired utterances. So, Paul reminds the Corinthians that one who speaks in tongues 'utters mysteries' (1 Cor. 14.2) and does not edify others (1 Cor. 14.4). For this reason, Paul insists that in the assembly 'he who prophesies is greater than one who speaks in tongues, unless he interprets' (1 Cor. 14.5). Finally, Paul concludes his attempt to redirect the Corinthians' approach toward the congregational use of tongues by laying down an important guideline: 'If anyone speaks in a tongue … someone must interpret' (1 Cor. 14.27). Indeed, 'If there is no interpreter, the speaker should keep quiet in the church and speak to himself and God' (1 Cor. 14.28).

Several important implications follow from these words of Paul. First, it must be emphasized that Paul does not envision the person who speaks in tongues to be in a state of ecstatic frenzy or unable to control his or her actions and speech. On the contrary, while the speaker may experience feelings of intense joy and be ushered by the Spirit into a state of spiritual rapture, this charismatic event does not involve the loss of control. The one who speaks in tongues, like the one who prophesies, is able to withhold or stop the utterance that is inspired by the Spirit. This remarkable interaction and cooperation of the divine and the human is what makes speaking in tongues, like all of the gifts of the Spirit, so special and mysterious. Note, however, that human consciousness is not lost as it meets the divine presence. At Pentecost each individual hears his or her own mother tongue and each person's unique, culturally conditioned identity is maintained (Acts 2.11). So also, when the Spirit inspires glossolalia, the tongues speaker's personality is respected and remains intact as the Spirit utters mysteries through us.

Second, here we encounter a theme that shapes and punctuates Paul's discussion throughout 1 Corinthians 12-14. Mutual edification is a central purpose for the expression of the gifts, at least in the corporate setting, and so it serves as a measuring stick, a means by which our actions may be directed and evaluated. This is precisely why love is so important if tongues and the other gifts are to be used as God intended (1 Corinthians 13).

Finally, we see here that Paul does envision a corporate expression of speaking in tongues. We have already noted that Paul encourages the churches at Ephesus and Colossae to sing in tongues (Eph. 5.19; Col. 3.16). We have also seen that speaking in tongues plays a positive role in corporate worship as a sign, a dramatic, tangible sign of God's presence in and his call upon the church (Acts 2.19, 33; 10.46; Mk 16.17; Rom. 8.26). Here, however, we see that Paul also anticipates that tongues might serve the community as a form of proclamation – as the means by which in dramatic fashion God speaks to the church.

Our conclusion that speaking in tongues together with interpretation might serve as proclamation requires some explanation. Many have maintained that in the New Testament speaking in tongues is always presented as praise, petition, or intercession addressed to God. Tongues, it is claimed, are never portrayed as a means by which God speaks to humans.[34] On this reading of 1 Corinthians 12-14, when Paul speaks of the interpretation of tongues, he refers to the interpretation of prayer or praise that is addressed to God. The notion of a message in tongues that is interpreted in a subsequent charismatic event and directed to the congregation in order to instruct, admonish, or edify is rejected as without biblical warrant. These scholars acknowledge that numerous Pentecostal churches claim to have experienced such charismatic messages. Nevertheless, they (at least the gracious ones) suggest that, rather than a 'message' in tongues with interpretation, in reality the two-fold charismatic event should be more properly described as an expression of glossolalic praise (directed to God), which is then followed by an unrelated word of prophecy (directed to the community).

I understand the thought process and arguments of these fine scholars. They probably represent the majority view on this issue. Nevertheless, I find this position overly rigid and ultimately unconvincing. I offer three reasons for my view, which does allow for the possibility that a message in tongues with interpretation might take the form of a word of instruction directed to the community.

First, a central plank in the argument built by those who advocate a more restrictive view (tongues are addressed only to God) is found in Paul's words in 1 Cor. 14.2: 'For anyone who speaks in a

---

[34] Stibbe, *Know Your Spiritual Gifts*, pp. 179-81.

tongue does not speak to men but to God. Indeed, no one understands him; he utters mysteries with his spirit.' Here it is claimed that Paul explicitly states that that tongues are directed 'to God' rather than 'to men'. Although this statement is formally correct, it misses the larger context and Paul's intent. Paul continues by stating his chief concern, 'Indeed, no one understands him …' (1 Cor. 14.2). The immediate context, then, as well as Paul's larger argument, suggests that the description of tongues as addressed 'not … to men but to God' (1 Cor. 14.2) serves to highlight their unintelligibility (only God understands them) rather than define the specific nature of their content (only praise addressed to God). This point is supported by the wording of Paul's command in 1 Cor. 14.28, 'If there is no interpreter, the speaker should keep quiet in the church and *speak to himself and God*'.[35] Obviously Paul's intent here is not to define the content of the message in tongues, for while praise should be addressed to God, it cannot be directed toward the speaker! Here, once again, we see that Paul's purpose is to highlight the unintelligibility of tongues (and hence the need for interpretation) rather than its content.

Second, I believe that Luke's description of the miraculous 'speaking in tongues' in Acts 2.11 also supports my case. Luke's account in Acts 2 highlights the missiological significance of the Pentecostal gift. He skillfully integrates the list of nations into his narrative and in this way stresses what is central: the gift of the Spirit enables the disciples to communicate with people 'from every nation under heaven' (Acts 2.5). The result of this divine enabling should not be understood simply as praise directed to God. It is, above all, proclamation. This is suggested by the language miracle and confirmed by the content of the inspired speech, 'the wonders of God' (τὰ μεγαλεῖα τοῦ θεοῦ; Acts 2.11). In the LXX this phrase (τὰ μεγαλεῖα τοῦ θεοῦ) is usually connected with verbs of proclamation and, as such, is addressed to people. This focus on the impact that the glossolalic utterances have on the hearers present is also maintained in Acts 10.46, even though tongues speech is here linked to 'praising God'. Here we see that Peter and his colleagues 'were astonished' by the tongues speech of the Gentiles and, as a result, recognized that they could not withhold water baptism from

---

[35] The italics are mine.

them (Acts 10.45-48). Additionally, in Acts 19.6 tongues are paired with prophecy, which elsewhere in Luke–Acts is almost always directed toward people.[36] All of this suggests that tongues speech may take the form of proclamation as well as praise; and, in either case, may be uttered primarily for the sake of other people present.[37]

Finally, in Col. 3.16, a text which, as we have seen, refers to singing in tongues, the singing of 'spiritual songs' is pictured as one way that the Colossians might 'teach and admonish one another'. Although exactly how this might take place is not explicitly stated, it is likely that Paul had in mind the interpretation of tongues or glossolalic singing in concert with intelligible singing and proclamation so that its essential meaning is transparent. In any event, here too we see that the impact of tongues upon the Christian community is highlighted, regardless of whether the specific content features praise, thanksgiving, or instruction.

These points suggest that we should not be too quick to assume that all forms of tongues speech must be addressed to God. Although I would acknowledge that the evidence indicates that speaking in tongues generally takes the form of inspired praise or thanksgiving, I am reluctant to limit its expression exclusively to speech directed toward God in a rigid fashion. This seems to read too much into Paul's words in 1 Cor. 14.2 and ignore evidence found elsewhere in both the writings of Luke and Paul.

What, then, shall we make of Paul's guidelines in 1 Cor. 14.27-28?

> If anyone speaks in a tongue, two – or at the most three – should speak, one at a time, and someone must interpret. If there is no interpreter, the speaker should keep quiet in the church and speak to himself and God (1 Cor. 14.27-28).

We have already emphasized that Paul's directives here need to be viewed in light of the larger context of his writings and with sensitivity to the fact that he is seeking to bring order to a chaotic and

---

[36] Note, for example, how the inspired utterances in Luke's infancy narratives are generally given in the 3rd person (Lk. 1.46-55, 67-75; 2.33-35); and, if given in the 2nd person, they are usually directed to people not to God (Lk. 1.42-45, 76-79). The one exception, Simeon's outburst of praise in Lk. 2.29-32, should probably be understood as both praise and proclamation.

[37] So also Flattery, *Spiritual*, p. 142.

abusive situation. For this reason, I would not press his command to limit tongues in the corporate setting only to those instances where interpretation accompanies the utterance. There are other expressions of speaking in tongues that appear to fall outside of Paul's intended scope here. These would include singing and, at times, praying in the Spirit in the context of corporate worship. The key here is that these expressions of tongues should not be disruptive of intelligible proclamation or teaching, should be subject to the leadership of the church, and thus should be done at appropriate times designated by church leaders. However, I would suggest that Paul's limitation of the public expression of tongues with interpretation to two or three instances in any given service serves a valuable purpose. It insures that speaking in tongues will not dominate our worship services and eclipse other elements vital to spiritual vitality and edification: prophecy, proclamation, and instruction.[38] Although it is perhaps possible that Paul would not be so restrictive in other settings where the abuse of tongues is not a significant problem, it is probably better to err on the side of caution on this matter. We will do well to follow strictly Paul's guidelines at this point. This will safeguard our worship services from confusion and chaos.

Conclusion

All of this adds up to a very positive resume for the gift of tongues, if not for the church at Corinth. At Corinth we must not confuse the problem of application with the gift itself. And we must also be sensitive to and learn from Paul's allusions to speaking in tongues outside of 1 Corinthians. Although the gift of tongues, like so many of God's rich blessings, can be abused, it is nevertheless a beautiful gift from God full of rich blessing (cf. Lk. 11.13). This too Paul clearly affirms.

We have seen that Paul understands speaking in tongues typically to be spontaneous, Spirit-inspired prayer. This special type of un-intelligible, charismatic prayer often takes the form of praise and

---

[38] As George Flattery notes, the main point of Paul's guidelines in 1 Cor. 14.27-28 is 'that there should be balanced participation' (Flattery, *The Holy Spirit in Your Life: A Systematic Approach to a Vibrant Relationship* [Springfield, MO: Network211, 2012], p. 116).

thanksgiving directed to God; however, these utterances may also give voice to intercessory prayer, as the Spirit prays for us and through us. Paul understands that this kind of charismatic prayer will normally take place in private settings, not during corporate worship. This appears to be his own practice and this is what he advocates for the church at Corinth. However, it should be noted that Paul's exhortations concerning singing in the Spirit (Eph. 5.19; Col. 3.16) call for a corporate expression of glossolalia. The more restrictive approach to this practice which Paul articulates in 1 Cor. 14.15-17 clearly does not represent his normal practice. Paul's dismissal of glossolalic praise in the corporate setting as not edifying for those who do not understand (1 Cor. 14.17) must be seen as a part of his attempt to correct the misunderstanding and abuses present at Corinth (cf. 14.23-25). These directives, then, although they are often taken as normative guidelines for 'church order' in contemporary worship settings, in reality represent extreme measures designed by Paul to combat a very specific, blatant, and egregious abuse. If at Corinth speaking in tongues had not posed the very real danger of eclipsing intelligible proclamation and instruction, and if at Corinth glossolalia had not been falsely exalted as a sign of 'maturity' and 'power', it is highly unlikely that Paul would have taken the strongly negative approach to the congregational use of tongues that he does in 1 Corinthians 14. This conclusion is not only supported by Paul's positive exhortations for believers to sing in the Spirit in Eph. 5.19 and Col. 3.16,[39] but by other passages which imply a corporate knowledge of speaking in tongues (Rom. 8.26; 1 Thess. 5.19; and Jude 20). In spite of this polemical context, Paul does sanction a public expression of tongues with interpretation (1 Cor. 14.27), but he is careful to limit its use and thereby provide important safeguards against chaos and confusion. While the public expression of the gift may include concert singing in tongues and times of corporate prayer, Paul thus also makes room for tongues and interpretation to function in a manner similar to that of prophecy in the gathered assembly (1 Cor. 14.5). The key, we have noted, is that the gift of tongues must be exercised in humility and with love. This indeed is 'the most excellent way' (1 Cor. 12.31).

---

[39] Paul's language in these verses, 'speak to one another' (Eph. 5.19) and 'teach and admonish one another' (Col. 3.16), demands a corporate setting.

Application

On December 9, 1982 Billy Graham delivered a sermon at Evangel College, the Assemblies of God's premier liberal arts institution.[40] Graham spoke at a special convocation that convened that day in the afternoon. A large group of university students, faculty, and guests from the community attended. Graham's visit generated a tremendous sense of excitement. The service lasted approximately an hour and was followed by a press conference.

By all accounts, Graham preached a wonderful sermon. However, his time was limited to about 30 minutes due to the preliminary prayers, hymns, and introductions. Professor Calvin Holsinger remarked, 'I noticed Dr. Graham occasionally looking at his watch, and that sort of intrigued me. He was getting sensitive, as I heard later, to the way time was going'.[41]

Robert Spence, then the President of Evangel College, describes what happened after Graham finished speaking:

At the end of Dr. Graham's message there was to be a choral response ... at the end of that they moved into kind of a worship chorus, a modulation of keys, and there was a spontaneous attitude and spirit of praise. It didn't have to be coached or directed by anyone. It was just spontaneous, and as this praise chorus or this musical expression was subsiding, a young man in the choir, whom I don't know, spoke ... This young man gave a message in tongues in a very clear articulation. It was unmistakably language in its development and orientation, not just a repetition of a few syllables.

At the conclusion of his message one of our pastors here in the city ... gave an interpretation. It was a profound message that he gave. There was no mistaking that here was a declaration, clearly outlining a message. There was content in what was being said. The sense that I think all of us had who understood Pentecostal

---

[40] The school is now known as Evangel University.

[41] Flower Pentecostal Heritage Center, 'Evangel College Oral History, November 27, 1991 interview of Prof. J. Calvin Holsinger by Steve Swingle', p. 3.

worship was that we had seen a very clear manifestation of the gift of tongues and the gift of interpretation.[42]

Samuel Kaunley, a Missouri State Trooper who was assigned to provide security for Billy Graham, shared his recollection of what transpired shortly after this event:

If I remember right, I heard Dr. Graham saying he had five points to preach. He had thirty minutes, and then there was a press conference right afterward. After the press conference, we got in the car ... I remember Dr. Graham saying to Tom Zimmerman, 'I have never felt the anointing to preach in any greater way in my entire life as I felt this day'.

Then he asked Dr. Grady [Wilson] if he recalled their conversations on the gift of tongues and prophecy and the Baptism of the Holy Spirit with the evidence of tongues. Dr. Grady [Wilson] said yes, and Billy Graham said, 'Well, I want you to consider something, Grady. I had five points and I had thirty minutes to preach. I preached three points, and at the end of three points I ran out of time, so ... I stopped. Immediately after I finished preaching there was a message in tongues given and interpretation, and the benediction. The thing I want you to consider was that point number four was the interpretation of the message in tongues verbatim, and point number five was the benediction'.[43]

This story illustrates beautifully how the Holy Spirit, through the gift of tongues in concert with the gift of interpretation, is able to communicate 'a profound message' to the Christian community.[44]

---

[42] Flower Pentecostal Heritage Center, 'Evangel College Oral History, December 10, 1991 interview of President Robert H. Spence by Steve Swingle', pp. 2-3.

[43] Flower Pentecostal Heritage Center, 'Evangel College Oral History, December 10, 1991 interview of Samuel M. Kaunley by Steve Swingle', pp. 2-3.

[44] Grant Wacker questions Sam Kaunley's interpretation of these events, especially Kaunley's claim that 'Graham vowed to reconsider his views about the Pentecostal teaching' (Kaunley does state that, 'Then Billy Graham turned to Dr. Zimmerman and said, "Tom, I'm going to go home and go into my office and get alone with God. The very first thing I'm going to ask God is, 'If there's something that You have for me that I haven't received or I haven't experienced yet, I want it, and I'm going to stay there until I get that answer'"'). Wacker offers two reasons for his guarded response: Graham did not mention this 'manifestly supernatural miracle' in the three other Assemblies of God events at which he

We should consider carefully the exegetical basis for any judgment that would prohibit this kind of 'message in tongues' from our worship services.

Reflection Questions

1. The author suggests that praying and singing in tongues were quite common in the early church. What evidence does he present to support this view? Do you agree?

2. Menzies also argues that praying and singing in tongues is edifying for Christians, even though they do not understand what they are saying. How does Menzies suggest that this unintelligible speech is edifying for us?

3. Various scholars assert that the groans of Rom. 8.26 refer to speaking in tongues. Menzies suggests that this has important implications for Pentecostal believers today. What are these important implications? Do you agree?

4. According to the author's reading of the New Testament, the gift of tongues, when used in conjunction with the gift of interpretation, can also be a means by which God speaks to his people. As such, these messages in tongues with interpretation may be addressed to the congregation rather than to God. What arguments does the author offer in support of this view?

5. According to Paul, in the corporate setting the gift of tongues must be exercised in humility and with love. What will this look like in my church?

---

spoke over the next day and a half; this response seems to be out of character with Graham's normal practice to refrain from taking 'a clear stand on such a controversial doctrine and practice' (Grant Wacker, *America's Pastor: Billy Graham and the Shaping of a Nation* [Cambridge, MA: The Belknap Press of Harvard University Press, 2014], p. 189). Yet Wacker's position seems unnecessarily negative and misses several important points: (1) arguments from silence are not very compelling; (2) Graham's purported statements to Grady Wilson are entirely consistent with Graham's theological perspective on tongues so clearly outlined by Wacker (Graham affirmed the gift for some; but rejected it as a sign available to all; see Wacker, *Billy Graham*, p. 188); and (3) Calvin Holsinger, Robert Spence, and Sam Kaunley all mention corroborating comments that Graham made some months later in a televised PTL interview that they observed (although Spence, unlike Holsinger and Kaunley, did not recall that in this interview Graham specifically referred to the 'message in tongues' as completing his sermon).

CONCLUSION:
THE VALUE OF TONGUES

By way of conclusion I would like to draw together the various insights that we have gleaned from the Gospel of Mark, Luke–Acts, and Paul's letters and form them into a series of brief theological reflections on the significance of the gift of tongues for contemporary Christian life. My reflections are structured around six central observations.

Tongues are a sign of our connection to the calling and power of the apostolic church.

The early Pentecostals loved the term, 'apostolic'. The Azusa Street revival (1906-1909), the chief catalyst for the modern Pentecostal movement, took place in the Apostolic Faith Mission. The key publication that heralded the news of this revival around the world was entitled, *The Apostolic Faith*. Pentecostals loved this term because it represented a conviction very dear to them: the experience and power of the apostolic church as described in the book of Acts are available today. Their experience is our experience. Their calling is our calling.

Our Pentecostal forefathers and foremothers not only understood this truth, but they experienced it. Speaking in tongues served as an important, experiential sign of their connection to the apostolic church. They read about these utterances inspired by the Holy Spirit in the biblical record, and then they experienced them. This was the demonstrative sign that encouraged them to cry out, '[We] have received the Holy Spirit just as [they] have' (Acts 10.47; cf. Acts 19.2, 6). For this reason, speaking in tongues might be viewed as a Pentecostal sacrament. It is an outward sign of a spiritual reality. It validates our approach to the Bible and our praxis, both of which are rooted in the conviction that the apostolic church should be our model.

This sense of connection to the calling and power of the apostolic church is greatly needed today. It serves as a much-needed corrective to traditional church life, which has far too often lost sight of the manifest presence of God. As traditional churches in the West have increasingly lost touch with the supernatural elements of the Christian faith, Pentecostals have reveled in their worship of an immanent God, a God who is truly with us – a God who speaks to us and through us. Although many in an increasingly secular West struggle to understand this kind of faith, Pentecostal churches around the world continue to grow at an amazing rate.[1]

Pentecostals are convinced that they stand on a strong biblical foundation when they highlight God's desire to speak to us and through us. Uncle Zheng stated it well, 'While we believe that the apostles are gone [limited to the Twelve]; the Spirit of the apostles is still the same'. Indeed, our experience of speaking in tongues confirms this. It also calls us to heed Zheng's warning, 'Acts is the pattern for the mission of the church. If the church does not follow the path of the early church, we will lose our way.'

Tongues also signify who we are: the end-time prophets that Joel anticipated.

As a sign of our connection to the apostolic church, speaking in tongues also calls us to embrace our true identity in Christ as end-time prophets (Acts 2.17-18). In Acts 2.17-18 (cf. Acts 2.4) speaking in tongues is specifically described as a fulfillment of Joel's prophecy that in the last days all of God's people will prophesy. When the Spirit fills Jesus' disciples and inspires their 'speaking in tongues', Peter explains the meaning of the discordant sounds to the amazed crowd. This cacophony is not the fruit of drunken revelry, far from it. Rather, it is the sound of inspired utterances issued by God's

---

[1] As we have noted, Philip Jenkins describes the Pentecostal movement as 'the most successful social movement of the past century' (Jenkins, *The Next Christendom*, p. 8).

end-time prophets (Acts 2.13, 15-17). The meaning of the symbolism of the speaking 'in other tongues', which enables 'the Jews from every nation under heaven' to hear the message in their 'own language', (Acts 2.5-6) is then clearly explained. The miraculous tongues mark this group as members of Joel's end-time prophetic band. They indicate that the 'last days' and the salvation associated with it have arrived. Peter also highlights the source of these inspired utterances, 'Exalted to the right hand of God ... he [Jesus] has poured out what you now see and hear' (Acts 2.33). These oracles uttered by the disciples of Jesus serve as proof that, 'God has made this Jesus ... both Lord and Christ' (Acts 2.36). Thus, in Acts 2 speaking in tongues is a sign that both validates the disciples' claim that Jesus is Lord and confirms their status as members of Joel's end-time prophetic band.

It is not without reason then that we Pentecostals appeal to Acts 2 as the template for our understanding of baptism in the Spirit as a prophetic and missiological enabling. The Pentecost story (Acts 2) shapes our experience and gives direction to our mission. Within the larger Christian family this emphasis is unique and it gives the Pentecostal movement a profoundly missional ethos.[2] This is undoubtedly one of the key reasons why Pentecostal churches are growing. It is certainly a central reason why scores of missionaries, most with meager financial backing, left the Azusa Street revival and traveled to diverse points of the globe to proclaim the apostolic faith. I would suggest it is also why Pentecostals today constantly share their faith with others. Bold witness for Jesus is recognized as our primary calling and the central purpose of our experience of the Spirit's power. Missions is woven into the fabric of our faith. And, it should be noted, speaking in tongues uniquely validates and symbolizes this prophetic and missiological understanding of the Pentecostal gift. This was true for the apostolic church. It is still true today.

---

[2] For more on this see Menzies, *Pentecost*, pp. 117-22 and Robert Menzies, 'Missional Spirituality: A Pentecostal Contribution to Spiritual Formation', in Teresa Chai (ed.), *A Theology of the Spirit in Doctrine and Demonstration: Essays in Honor of Wonsuk and Julie Ma* (Baguio City: APTS Press, 2014), pp. 39-56.

The diversity of tongues reminds us of the scope and nature of our mission.

In August of 2014 I was privileged to attend a worship service that formed the prelude to the Centennial Celebration of the Assemblies of God. This special worship service convened at my home church, Central Assembly of God in Springfield, Missouri. I arrived early, but found that I was already too late. The sanctuary was packed with people from 120 different nations. But I am not dissuaded easily, so I moved through the throng and attempted to locate a seat in the balcony. Over 3,500 packed into the church, which was filled with the chatter of languages from around the world. I found an empty spot in the aisle on the very top step of the balcony. To my immediate right was a young man from Bangladesh. In front of me was a Christian brother from Africa and to my left was a lady from Venezuela. It was a remarkable scene for Springfield, a rather small and monolithic community in the heart of the Midwest. I remember thinking that there is a lot of talk about diversity in the United States, but here you really have it. The media did not take much notice of this fact, but it was an amazing experience to hear the multiple languages around me as I entered and exited the sanctuary.

Yet the stunning diversity of the worshippers was not the only remarkable feature of this meeting. I found the unity that knit this diverse group together even more compelling and noteworthy. Here in the midst of this congregation representing seemingly 'every nation under heaven', there was a remarkable unity of faith and purpose. It was not a forced unity that destroys cultural distinctives and individual expression; rather, it was a beautiful unity of shared experience rooted in our common faith in Christ. Our mother tongues were different, but we all embrace the same gospel and worship the same Lord.

As I was taking all of this in from my perch on the top row of the balcony, my mind raced to the Pentecost account in Acts 2.4-11 and the list of nations recorded there. Dr. George Wood, the Assemblies of God General Superintendent, pointed out that just as there were 120 present at Pentecost (Acts 1.15), so also 120 nations were represented at this gathering. As I pondered this amazing fact and the account of Pentecost in Acts 2, two thoughts came to me.

First, it struck me that the extraordinary diversity of this multi-ethnic gathering and the emphasis on speaking in tongues that marks this Pentecostal group are not coincidental. As we have noted, speaking in tongues highlights the Holy Spirit's desire that all people – people from every language group – would have the opportunity to know and worship Jesus. Every time we speak in tongues or hear glossolalia in our worship services, it should remind us that God desires that every person on the planet should have the opportunity to hear the gospel. Every expression of tongues is a foretaste of our ultimate destiny which is so beautifully pictured in Revelation as members of a great choir comprised of worshippers from 'every nation, tribe, people, and language' who stand before the throne of God and declare praise to the Lamb (Rev. 7.9-12). As such, these experiences call us to work toward the fulfillment of this great vision. In other words, speaking in tongues and a concern for the 'unreached' of our world go hand in hand. I would suggest that this is a key, although often unarticulated, reason why Pentecostal churches have been such a powerful force in world missions over the last century. Our experience of glossolalia, like the tongues speech in Acts 2, represents an enacted parable that reminds us of our true calling and ultimate destiny.

My second thought flowed from and stood in contrast to the first. In the midst of the beautiful unity of faith and purpose reflected in our corporate worship, there was at the same time a wonderful diversity. Again, I was reminded of the Pentecost event. The disciples of Jesus who were 'filled with the Holy Spirit and began to speak in other tongues' (Acts 2.4) did not speak a single tongue that all understood. Rather, they spoke in the multiple mother tongues of each individual present. The cultural distinctives were not obliterated.[3] On the contrary, the Holy Spirit enabled Jesus' disciples to embrace them and minister through them. There were many languages, but only one message. And the message was simply this: Jesus is the resurrected and exalted Lord and only Jesus is worthy of our praise and worship (Acts 2.33).

So also today we have a clear message and a mandate to take the gospel of Jesus Christ to the ends of the earth. Every time the Holy

---

[3] Frank Macchia notes that Luke's presentation of tongues at Pentecost (Acts 2) 'resists making any single language or idiom absolute' (Macchia, *Baptized in the Spirit: A Global Pentecostal Theology* [Grand Rapids: Zondervan, 2006], p. 36).

Spirit inspires an utterance in tongues, this event serves to remind us of the incredible scope of our mission. Additionally, the fact that the Spirit inspires multiple and diverse tongues – indeed tongues unknown to us – this fact also encourages us to recognize that we are called to identify with and embed ourselves within the cultures of the peoples we seek to reach. In short, we must, like Jesus, become incarnate. This is the nature of our mission and our experience of tongues clarifies and reinforces this fact.

The intimacy of tongues reminds us that God is with us.

Many struggle with the notion that unintelligible speech can be edifying and useful. Yet there are numerous examples of that which transcends rational description or understanding serving as a powerful vehicle of communication and an effective means of expressing emotions. Poetry and music in particular come to mind. There is, however, perhaps an even closer and better analogy for tongues. The term 'idiolect' may be used to describe an intimate language that is only understood and shared by a select few.[4] Twins in infancy, for example, often use a language all their own. Only they can communicate by means of this idiolect. The use of an idiolect implies familiarity, trust, and intimacy. A number of biblical passages support this description of glossolalia as a kind of idiolect.

We have noted Luke's striking description of Jesus 'rejoicing in the Holy Spirit' and bursting forth in praise (Lk. 10.21). I have argued that Luke and his readers understood these words, particularly in light of the linguistic and thematic connections with Acts 2.26, to include glossolalia. It is noteworthy that immediately after this charismatic introduction, Jesus utters one of the most dramatic and intimate declarations contained in the synoptic gospels. This declaration highlights Jesus' unique relationship to the Father and his lofty status as the Son (Lk. 10.21-22). This suggests that glossolalia is indeed a language of intimacy.

---

[4] Simon Chan uses the term with respect to lovers who speak 'sweet nothings' that only they understand (Chan, 'The Language Game of Glossolalia, or Making Sense of the "Initial Evidence"', in Wonsuk Ma and Robert Menzies (eds.), *Pentecostalism in Context: Essays in Honor of William W. Menzies* [JPTSup 11; Sheffield: Sheffield Academic Press, 1997], pp. 85-86).

This judgment finds further support in the many references we have considered that present tongues as a form of doxological prayer.[5] These texts, which describe the Spirit praying through the believer, link speaking in tongues with a strong sense of communion with Christ. This is perhaps most beautifully expressed in the Abba prayer of Rom. 8.15-16 and Gal. 4.6. Paul declares that, 'the Spirit himself testifies with our spirit that we are God's children' (Rom. 8.16). While the Abba prayer references charismatic prayer more broadly, it clearly includes glossolalic prayer. Furthermore, Paul's words here paint a powerful picture of what happens as the Spirit prays through us. We are caught up in the love of Christ and filled with joy as we begin to glimpse the significance of our divine adoption. Is it any wonder that human words fail to express adequately what we feel?

Tongues, like an idiolect shared by twins, is an ongoing reminder of our close, filial relationship to God in Christ. It is a reminder that is made possible by the inspiration of the Holy Spirit and expressed in a form of intimate language. Jesus, here, is our model (Lk. 10.21).

The strangeness of tongues reminds us of our need to rely on the Holy Spirit.

In addition to this Spirit-inspired awareness of our filial relationship to God, Paul envisions another kind of realization that will produce glossolalia. This is the realization of our utter weakness that he describes so clearly in Rom. 8.18-27. The unintelligibility of tongues at this point is ironically meaningful. As Dunn observes, 'Here again we see the two sides of charismatic consciousness ... the consciousness of human impotence and the consciousness of divine power in and through that weakness'.[6] Our inability to know how or what to pray is a stark reminder of our weakness. It is a symptom of our present location in salvation history, looking toward the completion of that which has already begun. So, 'the Spirit himself intercedes for us with groans that words cannot express' (Rom. 8.26). We long for the transformation that is anticipated by the

---

[5] 1 Corinthians 12.2-3, 14.14-17; Rom. 8.15-16; Gal. 4.6; Eph. 5.18-19, 6.18; Col. 3.16; 1 Thess. 5.19; and Jude 20.

[6] Dunn, *Jesus and the Spirit*, p. 242.

presence of the Holy Spirit in our lives. And yet our weakness is all too clear. We realize that we cannot begin to express the longings and desires that the Spirit has birthed in our hearts. We sense that we are incapable of comprehending God's holiness and love. We do not know how to pray for our own needs or the needs of others.

Yet, in the midst of our weakness, the Spirit intercedes for us and through us, utilizing words that have no meaning to us. Our speech reflects our yearning and thus emerges as 'groans'. In the midst of this travail we come to an incredible awareness – a recognition that God is present in our weakness and accomplishing through us that which we cannot comprehend but sense to be precisely what we need. This is what makes the groans of Rom. 8.26 so edifying and so special. Here Paul helps us see that our experience of tongues is a mark of our weakness, a sign that we are utterly dependent. Nevertheless, as we have seen, it is also a sign of God's presence and power. The Spirit reminds us that we are being 'transformed into his likeness with ever-increasing glory' (2 Cor. 3.18). Clearly, there is a wonderful dialectic here.

The recognition that glossolalia serves as a sign of our weakness, as well as a sign of God's presence, carries with it significant implications for the contemporary church. First and foremost, it should help Pentecostals avoid the spurious notion that glossolalia is a sign of our maturity and our strength. We Pentecostals rightly celebrate the fact that Jesus has ushered in the Kingdom of God. However, we must also acknowledge that his Kingdom has not yet fully arrived. Of course, we too have not yet arrived. We are in the midst of a glorious process of transformation through the power of the Holy Spirit. Nevertheless, as Paul so descriptively states, 'we have this treasure in jars of clay' (2 Cor. 4.7). Our groaning serves to remind us that we are still largely clay.

Second, this awareness that tongues signify our weakness (as well as God's powerful presence) might serve to call an increasingly affluent and seemingly self-reliant church in the United States back to its roots. Historically, we Pentecostals have been people with little to lose. As a result, we have been desperate for God. Globally, the majority of Pentecostals still live on the wrong side of the tracks:

they are the poor, the powerless, and the marginalized.[7] So, they are hungry for God. And so, too, they recognize that they are absolutely dependent upon him. Pentecostals talk about God's power because they know that they are weak. They pray for God's healing and deliverance because they have no other hope. They seek God's presence because only in him do they find joy and peace. In a word, Pentecostals are desperate. Perhaps we who have lost our sense of desperation can find it once again as we cry out to God through the Spirit with groans.

The drama of tongues reminds us that a transcendent God delights to communicate with us.

Anyone who has participated in a Pentecostal worship service that has included people collectively praying or singing in tongues will attest to the fact that this expression of tongues adds a distinctly dramatic element to the worship service. This is equally true of those moments when the Spirit inspires a 'message' in tongues with interpretation. The spontaneous and striking quality of these experiences is unmistakable. Pentecostals recognize these moments as dramatic encounters with God. As Turner notes, in these moments glossolalic utterances verge on 'the theophanic and mystical'.[8] Samarin states it well when he declares, 'Tongues says "God is here", in the same way a Gothic cathedral says "God is majestic"'.[9] Indeed, there is an undeniable dramatic quality about tongues that signals to the gathered community that God is present and that he desires to communicate with us.

This dramatic quality of tongues reminds us that glossolalia is a theophany, a concrete manifestation of God's presence in our

---

[7] David Martin states, 'We have in Pentecostalism and all its associated movements the religious mobilization of the culturally despised, above all in the non-western world, outside any sponsorship whatever, whether of their own local intelligentsias, or of the clerical and secular intelligentsias of the West' (*Pentecostalism: The World Their Parish* [Oxford: Blackwell, 2002], p. 167).

[8] Turner, *Spiritual Gifts*, p. 311.

[9] W.J. Samarin, *Tongues of Men and Angels: The Religious Language of Pentecostalism* (London: Collier-Macmillan, 1972), pp. 154, 232, cited by both Turner, *Spiritual Gifts*, p. 312 and Macchia, 'Sighs', p. 53.

midst.[10] This point is highlighted in Acts 2.3-4, where at Pentecost the 'tongues of fire' (γλῶσσαι ὡσεὶ πυρός) are linked with 'speaking in tongues' (λαλεῖν ἑτέραις γλώσσαις). Although many scholars have attempted to connect the Pentecost account with Jewish Sinai traditions and in this way describe Pentecost as 'a new Sinai', elsewhere I have shown that these arguments miss the mark at every point.[11] First, it should be noted that Luke does not present the Pentecostal gift of the Spirit as the power of the new law of Christ; rather, according to Luke, 'the Spirit of Pentecost is the source of prophetic inspiration and, as such, the Spirit of mission'.[12] Additionally, the general parallels between the Pentecost account and the Sinai traditions do not suggest that Luke's narrative was influenced by these traditions. Rather, these parallels merely reflect the language commonly used to describe this kind of marvelous theophany. Numerous accounts in the Old Testament and other Jewish traditions describe God's manifest presence utilizing similar language. Terms such as 'wind', 'fire', 'word', and 'voice', are found in many descriptions of God's manifest presence or self-revelation.[13] These accounts of striking manifestations of God's presence remind us that God delights to communicate with us, and that he often does so in concrete and dramatic ways.

A particularly well-known theophany is described in 1 Kings 18. In response to Elijah's prayer, 'the fire of the Lord fell and burned up the sacrifice, the wood, the stones and the soil, and also licked up the water in the trench' (1 Kgs 18.38). The people's response is immediate: '... they fell prostrate and cried, 'The Lord – he is God!" (1 Kgs 18.39). Here, like at the burning bush (Exod. 3.2-6), God's powerful presence is revealed with fire.

God's presence is also manifest in a clear and compelling way in the fire that marked Solomon's dedication of the temple. At the close of Solomon's prayer of dedication, 'fire came down from

---

[10] Frank Macchia helpfully highlights this point, see Macchia, 'Sighs', pp. 54-57.

[11] See Menzies, *Empowered*, pp. 189-96 and the scholars cited there.

[12] Menzies, *Empowered*, p. 201. Note Peter's explicit description of this event as the fulfillment of Joel's prophecy (Acts 2.16-21).

[13] For example see 2 Sam. 22.8-15 and Isa. 66.15-16. For similar descriptions in Jewish traditions outside of the Protestant Bible, see *1 Enoch* 14.8-25; and *4 Ezra* 13.1-10.

heaven and consumed the burnt offering and the sacrifices, and the glory of the Lord filled the temple' (2 Chron. 7.1). Again, the people's response to this dramatic display of God's powerful presence is immediate: 'When all the Israelites saw the fire coming down … they knelt on the pavement with their faces to the ground, and they worshiped and gave thanks to the Lord …' (2 Chron. 7.3).

At Pentecost the dramatic events – rushing wind, tongues of fire, and inspired speech – also elicit responses from the crowd. Initially, the crowd is amazed and confused (Acts 2.12-13). However, after Peter's sermonic explanation of these events, 'they were cut to the heart' and asked, 'what shall we do?' (Acts 2.37). Thus, 'three thousand were added to their number that day' (Acts 2.41).

We should note that prophetic speech itself can function as a kind of theophany. Roger Stronstad and Wonsuk Ma have highlighted the fact that Spirit-inspired speech often serves to authenticate God's presence in and his call upon the life of an individual.[14] A classic example of this sort of prophetic theophany is found in the description of Saul's anointing and confirmation as king. Samuel declares that one of the 'signs' that will authenticate Saul's leadership and signify that 'God is with you' (1 Sam. 10.7) will be prophetic inspiration: 'The Spirit of the Lord will come upon you in power, and you will prophesy with [the prophets]; and you will be changed into a different person' (1 Sam. 10.6). Samuel's words are fulfilled, for the Spirit comes upon Saul and he immediately bursts forth with prophetic speech. The significance of Saul's ecstatic speech is not missed by the crowd. 'When all those who had formerly known [Saul] saw him prophesying with the prophets, they asked each other, "What is this that has happened to the son of Kish? Is Saul also among the prophets?"' (1 Sam. 10.11). Stronstad correctly notes that Saul's prophetic speech serves as a sign in two distinct ways. First, it signals to Saul that God is with him. Second, it demonstrates to the nation that Saul is the Lord's chosen leader.[15]

It would appear that Pentecostals stand on a firm, biblical foundation when they view speaking in tongues as a special kind of theophany. Like Elijah's fire and Saul's prophecy, glossolalia is a con-

---

[14] Stronstad, *Theology of St. Luke*, pp. 21-22; Ma, 'The Spirit of God upon Leaders of Ancient Israelite Society and Igorot Tribal Churches', pp. 292-302.
[15] Stronstad, *Theology of St. Luke*, p. 22.

crete manifestation of God's presence in our midst. As a type of Spirit-inspired speech (Acts 2.4, 17-21), it signifies in dramatic fashion that God delights to communicate with us and through us. In this way, speaking in tongues validates our proclamation about God and authenticates our calling by him. Is it any wonder that in a world desperately seeking for the God of the Bible who speaks and acts that the theophany of tongues has impacted the lives of so many? Is it any wonder that the theophany of tongues has served as a catalyst for renewal in churches that far too often have lost sight of the manifest presence of God?

Come, Holy Spirit, fill us. Inspire our tongues so that we might burst forth in praise to Jesus and bear bold witness for Him to the world.

BIBLIOGRAPHY

Anderson, Hugh, *The Gospel of Mark* (New Century Bible Commentary; Grand Rapids: Eerdmans, 1976).

Banks, Robert, *Paul's Idea of Community* (Grand Rapids: Eerdmans, 1980).

Barrett, C.K., *The Acts of the Apostles, Vol. 1* (London: T&T Clark International, 1994 [2004 edn]).

Bauckham, Richard J., *Jude, 2 Peter* (WBC 50; Waco, TX: Word, 1983).

Black, C. Clifton, *Mark* (Abingdon NT Commentaries; Nashville: Abingdon Press, 2011).

Blomberg, Craig L., *The Historical Reliability of the Gospels* (Downers Grove, IL: InterVarsity Press, 2nd edn, 2007).

Bock, Darrell L., *Acts* (Baker Exegetical Commentary on the New Testament; Grand Rapids: Baker, 2007).

—*Proclamation from Prophecy and Pattern: Lucan Old Testament Christology* (JSNTSS 12; Sheffield: JSOT Press, 1987).

Brown, S., '"Water-Baptism" and "Spirit-Baptism" in Luke–Acts', *ATR* 59 (1977), pp. 135-51.

Büchsel, F., *Der Geist Gottes im Neuen Testament* (Güttersloh: C. Bertlesmann, 1926).

Bultmann, Rudolph, 'New Testament and Mythology', in *Kerygma and Myth: A Theological Debate by Rudolf Bultmann and Five Critics* (ed. H.W. Bartsch; New York: Harper & Row, 1961), pp. 1-44.

—'ἀγαλλιάομαι', *TDNT*, I, pp. 19-21.

Carson, D.A., *Showing the Spirit: A Theological Exposition of 1 Corinthians 12-14* (Grand Rapids: Baker, 1987).

Casey, Maurice, *Aramaic Sources of Mark's Gospel* (SNTS 102; Cambridge: Cambridge University Press, 1998).

Chan, Simon, 'The Language Game of Glossolalia, or Making Sense of the "Initial Evidence"', in Wonsuk Ma and Robert Menzies (eds.), *Pentecostalism in Context: Essays in Honor of William W. Menzies* (JPTSup 11; Sheffield: Sheffield Academic Press, 1997), pp. 80-95.

Cole, R. Alan, *The Gospel According to Mark: An Introduction and Commentary* (Tyndale NT Commentaries; Grand Rapids: Eerdmans, 2nd edn, 1989).

Collins, Adela Yarbro, *Mark: A Commentary* (Hermeneia; Minneapolis: Fortress Press, 2007).

Conzelmann, Hans, *Acts of the Apostles* (Philadelphia: Fortress Press, 1987; German original, 1963).

Croy, Clayton N., *The Mutilation of Mark's Gospel* (Nashville: Abingdon Press, 2003).

de Boor, Carl, *Neue Fragmente des Papias, Hegesippus und Pierius, in bischer unbekannten Excerpten aus der Kirchengeschichte des Philippus Sidetes* (TU 5.2; Leipzig: J.C. Hinrich, 1888).

Dunn, James D.G., *Jesus and the Spirit. A Study of the Religious and Charismatic Experience of Jesus and the First Christians as Reflected in the New Testament* (London: SCM Press, 1975).

Edwards, James R., *The Gospel According to Mark* (Pillar NT Commentary; Grand Rapids: Eerdmans, 2002).

Elbert, Paul, *Pastoral Letter to Theo: An Introduction to Interpretation and Women's Ministries* (Eugene, OR: Wipf & Stock, 2008).

Ellis, E. Earle, *The Gospel of Luke* (New Century Bible Commentary; Grand Rapids: Eerdmans, rev. edn, 1974).

Evans, Craig A., *Luke* (New International Biblical Commentary; Peabody: Hendrickson, 1990).

—*Mark 8.27-16.20* (Word Biblical Commentary 34b; Nashville: Thomas Nelson Publishers, 2001).

Evans, C.F., 'The Central Section of Luke's Gospel', in D.E. Nineham (ed.), *Studies in the Gospels* (Oxford: Blackwell, 1957), pp. 37-53.

Everts, Jenny, 'Tongues or Languages? Contextual Consistency in the Translation of Acts 2', *JPT* 4 (1994), pp. 71-80.

Fee, Gordon D., *The First Epistle to the Corinthians* (NICNT; Grand Rapids: Eerdmans, 1987).

—*God's Empowering Presence: The Holy Spirit in the Letters of Paul* (Peabody, MA: Hendrickson, 1994).

Fitzmyer, Joseph A., *The Gospel According to Luke, Vol. 2* (AB 28; New York: Doubleday, 1985).

—*The Acts of the Apostles* (The Anchor Yale Bible; New Haven, MA: Yale University Press, 1998).

Flattery, George M., *Spiritual Persons, Gifts, and Churches: A Commentary on 1 Corinthians 12-14* (Springfield, MO: Network211, 2015).

—*The Holy Spirit in Your Life: A Systematic Approach to a Vibrant Relationship* (Springfield, MO: Network211, 2012).

Forbes, Christopher, *Prophecy and Inspired Speech in Early Christianity and its Hellenistic Environment* (Tübingen: Mohr, 1995).

Forbes, Greg W., *The God of Old: The Role of the Lukan Parables in the Purpose of Luke's Gospel* (JSNTSS 198; Sheffield: Sheffield Academic Press, 2000).

Garland, David, *1 Corinthians* (Grand Rapids: Baker, Academic, 2003).

Geddert, Timothy J., *Mark* (Believers Church Bible Commentary; Scottdale, PA: Herald Press, 2001).

Graves, Robert W., *Praying in the Spirit* (Old Tappan, NJ: Chosen Books, 1987).

Green, Gene L., *Jude and 2 Peter* (ECNT; Grand Rapids: Baker Academic, 2008).

Green, Joel B., *The Gospel of Luke* (NICNT; Grand Rapids: Eerdmans, 1997).

Haenchen, Ernst, *The Acts of the Apostles* (Philadelphia: The Westminster Press, 1971).

Harvey, Robert and Philip H. Towner, *2 Peter and Jude* (IVP; Downers Grove, IL: InterVarsity Press, 2009).

Hovenden, Gerald, *Speaking in Tongues: The New Testament Evidence in Context* (JPTSup 22; London: Sheffield Academic Press, 2002).

Jenkins, Philip, *The Next Christendom: The Coming of Global Christianity* (Oxford: Oxford University Press, 2002).

Johanson, Bruce C., 'Tongues, a Sign for Unbelievers?', *NTS* 25 (1979), pp. 180-203.

Käsemann, Ernst, *Perspectives on Paul* (Philadelphia: Fortress Press, 1971).

—*Commentary on Romans* (Grand Rapids: Eerdmans, 1980).

Keener, Craig S., *Acts: An Exegetical Commentary, Vol. 1* (Grand Rapids: Baker Academic, 2012).

—*1-2 Corinthians* (New Cambridge Bible Commentary; Cambridge: Cambridge University Press, 2005).

—*Gift & Giver: The Holy Spirit for Today* (Grand Rapids: Baker, 2001).

Kelhoffer, James A., *Miracle and Mission: The Authentication of Missionaries and Their Message in the Longer Ending of Mark* (WUNT 2.112; Tübingen: Mohr Siebeck, 2000).

Kistemaker, S.J., *1 Corinthians* (Grand Rapids: Baker, 1993).

Longenecker, Richard N., *Biblical Exegesis in the Apostolic Period* (Grand Rapids: Eerdmans, 2nd edn, 1999).

Luz, Ulrich, 'Paul as Mystic', in *The Holy Spirit and Christian Origins: Essays in Honor of James D.G. Dunn* (ed. Graham N. Stanton, Bruce W. Longenecker, and Stephen C. Barton; Grand Rapids:. Eerdmans, 2004), pp. 131-43.

Ma, Wonsuk, 'The Spirit of God upon Leaders of Ancient Israelite Society and Igorot Tribal Churches', in Wonsuk Ma and Robert Menzies (eds.), *Pentecostalism in Context: Essays in Honor of William W. Menzies* (JPT Sup 11; Sheffield: Sheffield Academic Press, 1997), pp. 291-316.

Macchia, Frank D., 'Sighs too deep for Words: Toward a Theology of Glossolalia', *Journal of Pentecostal Theology* 1 (1992), pp. 47-73.

—*Baptized in the Spirit: A Global Pentecostal Theology* (Grand Rapids: Zondervan, 2006).

Marcus, Joel, *Mark 8-16* (The Anchor Yale Bible 27A; New Haven: Yale University Press, 2009).

Marshall, I. Howard, *The Gospel of Luke: A Commentary on the Greek Text* (NIGTC; Grand Rapids: Eerdmans, 1978).

—*Luke: Historian and Theologian* (Carlisle, UK: Paternoster, 1988).

—'Acts', in G.K. Beale and D.A. Carson (eds.), *Commentary on the New Testament Use of the Old Testament* (Grand Rapids: Baker Academic, 2007), pp. 513-606.

Martin, David, *Pentecostalism: The World Their Parish* (Oxford: Blackwell, 2002).

May, Jordan, *Global Witness to Pentecost: The Testimony of 'Other Tongues'* (Cleveland, TN: Cherohala Press, 2013).

Menzies, Robert, *Empowered for Witness: The Spirit in Luke–Acts* (JPTSS 6; Sheffield: Sheffield Academic Press, 1994).

—*The Development of Early Christian Pneumatology with Special Reference to Luke–Acts* (JSNTS 54, Sheffield: JSPT Press, 1991).

—*The Language of the Spirit: Interpreting and Translating Charismatic Terms* (Cleveland, TN: CPT Press, 2010).

—'The Sending of the Seventy and Luke's Purpose', in Paul Alexander, Jordan D. May, and Robert Reid (eds.), *Trajectories in the Book of Acts: Essays in Honor of John Wesley Wyckoff* (Eugene, OR: Wipf & Stock, 2010), pp. 87-113.

—'The Persecuted Prophets: A Mirror-Image of Luke's Spirit-Inspired Church', in I. Howard Marshall, Volker Rabens, and Cornelis Bennema (eds.), *The Spirit and Christ in the New Testament & Christian Theology* (Grand Rapids: Eerdmans, 2012), pp. 52-70.

—*Pentecost: This Story Is Our Story* (Springfield, MO: GPH, 2013).

—*Making Pentecost Your Story: 50 Days of Reflection and Prayer – A Devotional Companion for* Pentecost: This Story Is Our Story *Inspired by the Church in China* (Xanesti eBook, 2015).

—'Evidential Tongues: An Essay on Theological Method', *Asian Journal of Pentecostal Studies* 1 (1998), pp. 111-23.

—'Missional Spirituality: A Pentecostal Contribution to Spiritual Formation', in Teresa Chai (ed.), *A Theology of the Spirit in Doctrine and Demonstration: Essays in Honor of Wonsuk and Julie Ma* (Baguio City: APTS Press, 2014), pp. 39-56.

Menzies, William and Robert, *Spirit and Power: Foundations of Pentecostal Experience* (Grand Rapids: Zondervan, 2000).

Metzger, Bruce, 'Seventy or Seventy-Two Disciples?', *NTS* 5 (1959), pp. 299-306.

—*The Text of the New Testament* (New York: Oxford, 1964).

Minear, Paul S., *To Heal and To Reveal: The Prophetic Vocation According to Luke* (New York: The Seabury Press, 1976).

Mosessner, David P., *Lord of the Banquet: The Literary and Theological Significance of the Lukan Travel Narrative* (Minneapolis: Fortress Press, 1989).

Mosessner, David P., 'Two Lords 'at the Right Hand'? The Psalms and an Intertextual Reading of Peter's Pentecost Speech (Acts 2.14-36)', in Richard Thompson and Thomas Phillips (eds.), *Literary Studies in Luke–Acts: Essays in Honor of Joseph B. Tyson* (Macon, GA: Mercer University Press, 1998), pp. 215-32.

Montague, George T., *The Holy Spirit: Growth of a Biblical Tradition* (New York: Paulist Press, 1976).

Morrice, W.G., *Joy in the New Testament* (Exeter: Paternoster Press, 1984).

Nickle, Keith F., *Preaching the Gospel of Luke: Proclaiming God's Royal Rule* (Louisville: Westminster John Knox Press, 2000).

Nolland, J., *Luke 9.21-18.34* (Word Biblical Commentary 35B; Dallas, TX: Word, 1993).

Ramsay, William M., *St. Paul the Traveller and Roman Citizen* (ed. Mark Wilson; Grand Rapids: Kregel, 2001 [orig. 1895]).

Samarin, W.J., *Tongues of Men and Angels: The Religious Language of Pentecostalism* (London: Collier-Macmillan, 1972).

Schweizer, Eduard, 'πνεῦμα', *TDNT*, VI, pp. 389-455.

Shogren, Gary S., 'The Gift of Tongues in the Post-Apostolic Church: A Rejoinder to Cleon Rogers', in Robert W. Graves (ed.), *Strangers to Fire: When Tradition Trumps Scripture* (Woodstock, GA: The Foundation for Pentecostal Scholarship, 2014), pp. 399-410.

Smith, James K.A., *Thinking in Tongues: Pentecostal Contributions to Christian Philosophy* (Grand Rapids: Eerdmans, 2010).

Stibbe, Mark, *Know Your Spiritual Gifts: Practising the Presents of God* (London: Marshall Pickering, 1997).

Stronstad, R., *The Charismatic Theology of St. Luke* (Peabody, MA: Hendrickson, 1984).

Sweet, J.P.M., 'A Sign for Unbelievers: Paul's Attitude to Glossolalia', in Watson E. Mills (ed.), *Speaking in Tongues: A Guide to Research on Glossolalia* (Grand Rapids: Eerdmans, 1986), pp. 141-64.

Synan, Vinson, 'The Role of Tongues as Initial Evidence', in Mark Wilson (ed.), *Spirit and Renewal: Essays in Honor of J. Rodman Williams* (JPTSup 5; Sheffield: Sheffield Academic Press, 1994), pp. 67-82.

Tannehill, Robert C., *The Narrative Unity of Luke–Acts: A Literary Interpretation, Volume 1. The Gospel According to Luke* (Philadelphia: Fortress Press, 1986).

Thiselton, Anthony, *The First Epistle to the Corinthians* (Grand Rapids: Eerdmans, 2000).

Turner, Max, *The Holy Spirit and Spiritual Gifts Then and Now* (Carlisle, UK: Paternoster, 1996).

Turner, Max, 'Tongues: An Experience for All in the Pauline Churches?', *Asian Journal of Pentecostal Studies* 1 (1998), pp. 231-53.

Vinson, Richard, *Luke* (Macon, GA: Smyth & Helwys Publishing, 2008).

Wacker, Grant, *America's Pastor: Billy Graham and the Shaping of a Nation* (Cambridge, MA: The Belknap Press of Harvard University Press, 2014).

Wallace, Daniel, 'Mark 16:8 as the Conclusion to the Second Gospel', in David Alan Black (ed.), *Perspectives on the Ending of Mark* (Nashville: B&H Academic, 2008), pp. 1-39.

Wedderburn, A.J.M., 'Romans 8:26 – Towards a Theology of Glossolalia', *Scottish Journal of Theology* 28 (1975), pp. 369-77.

Wenham, Gordon, *Numbers: An Introduction and Commentary* (Tyndale OT Commentary Series; Downers Grove, IL: Inter-Varsity Press, 1981).

Witherington III, Ben, *The Acts of the Apostles: A Socio-Rhetorical Commentary* (Grand Rapids: Eerdmans, 1998).

Woods, Edward J., *The 'Finger of God' and Pneumatology in Luke–Acts* (JSNTSS 205; Sheffield: Sheffield Academic Press, 2001).

Yong, Amos, *The Spirit Poured Out on All Flesh: Pentecostalism and the Possibility of Global Theology* (Grand Rapids: Baker, 2005).

Index of Biblical (and Other Ancient) References

Index of Names

Made in the USA
Lexington, KY
03 April 2019